To Trudie from
Sherman's Edith —
Sherman is younger brother
of Florence.

Lotus Blossom
R E T U R N S

The Remarkable Life of Florence Nagel-Longway-Howlett

with Sandy Zaugg

Pacific Press® Publishing Association
Nampa, Idaho
Oshawa, Ontario, Canada
www.pacificpress.com

Designed by Dennis Ferree
Cover art by Justinen Creative Group ©

Additional copies of this book are available by calling toll free 1-800-765-6955
or by visiting http://www.adventistbookcenter.com

Library of Congress Cataloging-in-Publication Data

Howlett, Florence Ione, 1910-
Lotus blossom returns: the remarkable life of
Florence Nagel-Longway-Howlett/with Sandy Zaugg.
p. cm.
ISBN: 0-8163-2044-6
1. Howlett, Florence Ione, 1910- 2. Missionaries, Medical—Biography.
3. Missions, Medical—Thailand. 4. Missions, Medical—Viet Nam. 5. Missions,
Medical—Hong Kong (China) I. Zaugg, Sandra L., 1938- II. Title

R722.32H69A3 2005
610.63—dc22   2004054277

05 06 07 08 09 · 5 4 3 2 1

Dedication

To my father and mother, Sherman and Mary Nagel,
who, by their lives, inspired my life in early youth
to follow in their footsteps,
and to all of my Chinese friends who encouraged me
to return to China.—FLH

To my sister, Donna R. Jones, who is my chief cheerleader,
and who happily reads anything and everything that I write.
And to my Tuesday critique group
for guiding comments, unstinting encouragement,
and prayers.—SZ

Contents

CHAPTER ONE

Submarine to the Rescue

Pastor Sherman Nagel stood looking down at the bed—at the *two ladies now in his life. Dear Lord,* he prayed silently, *please bless this newborn baby. Help me to be a good father to her and a good husband to Mary.*

The brand-new mother smiled up at her husband. "Thank God this baby was born alive and healthy! Have you thought of a name? What shall we call her?"

"Florence," the new father responded immediately. "Florence Ione Nagel. How does that sound?"

"Florence. I like that." She looked down at the tiny newborn in her arms. "Well, little Florence, you were in a big hurry to see China, weren't you?"

Sherman laughed. "My head is still spinning! So much has happened to us during this last year. Some of it has been difficult, but God has indeed been good."

Mary Nagel yawned and swept her hair out of her eyes with a tired hand. "Florence is almost two months early," she said. "Perhaps she knows she's going to do great things for God, and she's eager to get started."

Sherman leaned down and kissed his wife. "Sleep now, my dear," he said. "Call if you need me." Then he touched the baby's cheek with his finger. "Well, Florence, your papa's got a sermon to prepare, but I won't be far away."

He left the room but didn't immediately set to work. First he wandered outside and sat down on the porch, letting his mind whirl back over the rapid events of the last year. It had all started with the telegram from his father. ARE YOU GOING TO CHINA STOP READ IT IN THE REVIEW AND HERALD STOP DAD.

Sherman and Mary had immediately grabbed the last copy of *The Review and Herald* and searched it. There it was—the announcement that they were going to be missionaries in China. But how could it be possible? Yes, they had expressed an interest in China, but they couldn't go right now. And yes, Sherman had taken the Medical Missionary Training Course at the medical school in Loma Linda, which taught him simple medical procedures and first aid just in case they ever did go to the mission field. Yes, he had even worked for a short time in the Young People's Department of their conference. But they'd just moved to Freewater, Oregon, and he was looking for work; Mary was expecting their first child. They couldn't travel with a newborn infant, could they? And China was so far away. Seven whole years was a long time to leave family and friends. No! They definitely couldn't go right now.

Where did the editor get his information, Sherman had wondered. The Seventh-day Adventist General Conference Mission Board had never contacted him. So it couldn't be true.

But a few days later an official letter had arrived informing Sherman and Mary that they were booked to sail on the SS *Monteagle,* leaving San Francisco in one month bound for China!

They had prayed earnestly to know God's will—and then had begun packing. During their farewell visit to Sherman's parents, Mary had given birth prematurely. The baby had lived only a few hours. Even now, twelve months later, Sherman felt an ache in his heart as he remembered. So it was with heavy hearts that Sherman and Mary Nagel had joined seventeen other missionaries on board the SS *Monteagle* on October 16, 1909, and sailed out of San Francisco through the Golden Gate that guarded the entrance to the bay. On November 14 the ship had anchored in Shanghai; they were met by Dr. Harry W. Miller, who had already been working in the remote interior of China for seven years.

The Nagels had spent the first few months studying the baffling tones of the Chinese language. But before they had a chance to master the language, they had found themselves once more on a ship, bound, this time, for Hong Kong.

There they had continued to study the language. Because they could still carry on only the simplest conversations in Chinese, Sherman had concentrated his work among the English-speaking population. He gave Bible studies and talked about Jesus all over the vast city. But living in Hong Kong had an added personal bonus for Sherman. His brother, Lee, was a businessman there, so they were able to spend time together. Soon Mary Nagel had become pregnant again. Six and a half months into her pregnancy, the hot sultry weather in Hong Kong had begun to affect her severely. Exhaustion almost overwhelmed her. So when the Nagels had an opportunity for a short rest in a beach cottage in Macau, a Portuguese protectorate near Hong Kong, they had gladly accepted it.

The first morning there—*Could it have been only this morning?* Sherman asked himself—Mary had awakened in severe pain. Sherman had called the only available physician in town, an elderly Portuguese man who couldn't speak English. Using sign language, the doctor had given instructions about the medication and had indicated that he would return about three o'clock to check on his patient.

Baby Florence Ione Nagel with her parents, Sherman and Mary Nagel. Florence was born October 16, 1910, in Macao, a Portuguese colony near Hong Kong.

Mary's pain had increased. Sherman had paced the floor and prayed. Was Mary about to give birth to their second baby two months early? What should he do? Would this baby die too? "Please, loving Father, let this baby live," he had prayed. Then he had swallowed the lump in his throat and added, "Thy will be done."

By the time the doctor had finally returned, a baby girl, weighing almost five pounds, had greeted him with a faint cry. Florence Ione Nagel had entered the world on the afternoon of October 16, 1910, just one year from the day her mother and father had set sail for China. It was a day her father would never forget.

It soon became apparent that the Chinese people couldn't pronounce such a strange name as Florence. Pastor Nagel spoke to his language teacher about it. "Learned teacher," he said in the polite Chinese style, "my daughter has a name too foreign for people to speak. Will you please choose a Chinese name for her?" Then the new father added, "*Florence* means 'blooming.' "

The teacher thought for a few moments before he answered. "I think," he said slowly, "that 'Fa Lien'

The Adventist mission compound in Wai Chow, 150 miles northeast of Canton where the Nagels moved shortly after Florence was born.

The mission compound sat on a strip of high ground between two rivers. Access to the town of Wai Chow was through this gate in the city wall—the "Convenient Gate."

would be a suitable name for such a tiny girl. In English it means 'Lotus Blossom.' "

Within a few months the Nagel family moved again, this time to a large new mission compound just outside the walled city of Wai Chow (why-jow), 150 miles northeast of Canton. Pastor J. P. Anderson and his new bride, Amanda, already lived there, working among the Chinese Hakka (ha-kah) people who lived in that part of the country. The compound lay on a strip of raised land between two rivers with access to the city through an entrance called Convenient Gate.

Florence's mother was excited. She and her husband had never been settled in any place more than a few months since they were married. On the mission compound, next to the Andersons' house, a home had been built for them—a wonderful, spacious new home with two floors and a basement. And it was ready for them to move into just as soon as their furniture arrived. The furniture was already in port in Canton. Sherman just needed to go down there and make arrangements to pick it up and have it transported to Wai Chow. While they waited, they stayed in the Andersons' home.

The Andersons soon left for a short vacation in Hong Kong. A few days later, Pastor Nagel kissed his wife goodbye and left for Canton. A strange feeling came over Mary. She and her baby were all alone—deep in the interior of China with no means of communication with the outside world. All she could do was to put her trust in her heavenly Father who had promised, "I will never leave you nor forsake you" (see Hebrews 13:5).

The boat Pastor Nagel boarded was a strange vessel called a *to dai* (toe-dye). A tugboat towed it up and down the river. It had two large eyes painted on the bow, and two large dragons decorated the stern—"to combat the forces of evil spirits," he was told. As Pastor Nagel stood on the deck, a cold wind whistled around him. His fur-lined overcoat felt good even with the sun shining. He stayed on deck for a while, enjoying the scenery.

About a third of the way through the journey, a shout from the river bank broke the calm stillness. "Pull over to the bank and stop!" ordered a gruff voice in Chinese.

Instead, the tugboat captain put on more steam, hoping to get away. The bandits raised their guns and shot at the *to dai*. Passengers fell to the deck and crawled for cover. The captain reluctantly ordered the boat pulled to shore, and the bandits climbed aboard. Then they began looting the passengers.

One held a gun to Pastor Nagel's face while another stripped him of his overcoat and shoes and all his money. The second group took his suit coat, pants, and shirt. A third group picked up his suitcase and rifled through it, removing whatever interested them. An hour later, at a shrill whistle from the bandit chief, the looters left the boat, burdened down with clothes, watches, money, and other valuables they had stolen from the passengers. By this time many of the women passengers were crying hysterically, and the children were screaming.

As Pastor Nagel sat shivering from cold and trembling from his first encounter with bandits, the tugboat captain approached him and told him that the passengers were all begging to return to Wai Chow. Sherman stood up straight and looked sternly at the captain. "No," he said firmly. "We must go on to Canton. It is closer than Wai Chow now."

So to Canton they went. When they finally arrived, the police were notified. As soon as he could, Pastor Nagel reported the experience to the American consulate. The consul informed him that he had heard rumors of an internal uprising in the present Chinese government and was just getting ready to send a bulletin to Wai Chow ordering all Americans out of that part of China for a period of time until the situation was safer.

"Where is your family?" the consul asked.

"In Wai Chow—all alone," the new father replied with a quivering voice.

"You must go back and bring out your wife and baby immediately," the consul ordered.

Pastor Nagel hired a rickshaw to take him to the Adventist mission compound in Tung Shan. He told the missionaries there about his frightening trip from Wai Chow. Having been in the country for several years, Pastor Edwin and Susan Wilbur were sympathetic. They, too, had experienced many harrowing times.

Pastor Nagel knew he must return to Wai Chow immediately. Return? The very thought of it caused his hands to tremble and cold sweat to stand out on his forehead.

Edwin Wilbur took one look at Pastor Nagel and said, "You're in no shape to go back up that river, Sherman. I've had more experience than you. I'll go bring your Mary and baby Florence to Canton."

In the meantime, in Wai Chow, Mary Nagel was beginning to worry. "Where is Sherman? Why doesn't he come?" Day after day she prayed while she paced the floor or rocked Florence.

Then one day the gateman came to tell her that a strange white man was at the gate asking for permission to come in. Going with the gateman, Mary was surprised to see Pastor Wilbur, a missionary she had met briefly when they had traveled through Canton.

"I've come to take you and your baby to Canton, Mrs. Nagel," he said. "The American consulate has given orders for all Americans to leave the interior."

"But why did *you* come?" she asked. "Where is my husband?" Her voice sounded desperate. "What has happened to him?"

"Nothing has happened to your husband," Pastor Wilbur assured her in a soft, soothing voice. "He was so tired when he got to Canton, I decided to come after you myself and let him rest. We must take the next boat back to Canton. Can you be ready to go right away?"

But no boats left Wai Chow. The shipping company had heard of the uprising and was afraid to send its boats down the river for fear they would be confiscated to transport soldiers. Days passed. Every day, the gateman went to the dock to check with the shipping company.

Finally one day the gateman returned with news: "Be at the dock by five o'clock tomorrow morning," he said.

Before daybreak the next morning, Pastor Wilbur took Mary Nagel, four-month-old Florence, and their few belongings down to the dock and aboard the boat.

Mary Nagel's stomach revolted when she sat down to the first breakfast on board. She looked at the watery rice gruel with hard-boiled duck eggs and the coarse, partially cooked greens, and quickly she excused herself. Fortunately, she had packed some food for baby Florence, and that would do just fine for her, too.

In Canton, Sherman became panicky as day after day passed with no word from Pastor Wilbur—and no sight of Mary and Florence. *Surely the robbers have kidnapped both of them,* he thought. Finally in desperation, he called on the American consulate once again. The consul was also worried and commanded an American submarine crew to go up the Pearl River and see what they could find out.

Just where the East River flows into the Pearl River, Pastor Wilbur stood on the top deck of the boat, watching a strange object in the distance. Squinting into the sunlight, he caught sight of an American flag! As it came nearer, he recognized it as the submarine that was usually anchored off the pier in front of the American consulate in Canton. Interested passengers crowded the deck of the *to dai,* watching this strange vessel flying a strange flag. This was as good as a festival!

The captain of the submarine commanded the *to dai* to stop. Then he bellowed, "Are any Westerners on board?"

Cheerfully the passengers pulled the Americans to the railing. The relieved submarine captain supervised the transfer of Mary, Florence, and Pastor Wilbur to his ship then delivered them safely to the consulate in Canton.

What a happy man Sherman Nagel was when he saw his wife and baby! He and Mary knelt down and thanked God for deliverance and for bringing them safely together again.

CHAPTER TWO

Life on the Compound

In 1911, the old dynasty was overthrown after ruling for centuries, and Dr. Sun Yat-sen became the new revolutionary leader of China. This change in leadership also brought an end to foot binding for infant girls, and men cut off their queues, which they had worn as a symbol of loyalty and subservience to the emperor. Turmoil continued in China for years. The new Nationalist Army and those still loyal to the old regime clashed frequently—and violently. Locally powerful warlords added to the chaos. However, within a month the political upheaval calmed enough for Pastor and Mrs. Nagel and baby Florence to venture back up the East River to Wai Chow, taking with them all the boxes and furniture that had come from America. It was an exciting time on the compound. The Nagels moved into their own home. Sherman and Mary thanked the Lord for Adventist believers back in America who had given their money so that the missionaries in Wai Chow could have real homes—not native huts like the earlier pioneers had lived in.

Yet, it still wasn't quite like home. They had no electricity, no running water, no telephone, and no flushing toilet—not even a bathroom. They had no refrigeration of any kind. Since the hot weather lasted nine months out of the year, this created quite a serious problem. Mary solved this problem herself. She ordered a box made with two shelves and covered it with a screen. Then she fastened a rope to the top of the box and lowered it twenty feet into the well where it hung just above the water. In this manner, their food kept cool and fresh.

Sherman ordered a cast-iron stove and an oven from a Sears & Roebuck catalog. Ordering home furnishings or clothes through either Montgomery Ward or Sears & Roebuck catalogs was convenient for missionaries. Shipping was cheap, and orders arrived within two months. Mary couldn't use her new stove and oven much during the long, hot months, however. Cooking on the cast-iron stove turned the whole house into a hot furnace.

Florence in 1912.

The Chinese Hakka people had a better idea. They located their kitchens in adjacent quarters outside their houses. And they arranged a system whereby cooking also heated water for their daily baths! Even during the hottest weather, a good Hakka took a hot bath every evening. Each bather used two buckets—one for hot water, one for cold. For a washcloth they used a towel no bigger than an American hand towel. Then they wrung the water from it and used it as a towel to dry themselves. As the water evaporated from their slightly damp bodies, they felt cool!

Over the next few years, the Nagels' admiration for the ingenuity of the Hakka people grew, and they copied many of their ideas. Sherman had a room built against the outside of their home to be used for cooking, washing clothes, and as a primitive bathroom. For washing clothes, he ordered two large galvanized tubs and a tin clothes boiler from Sears & Roebuck. In the winter he brought one of the washtubs into the kitchen for the family baths.

Adjusting to native food was hard at first for Mary. It didn't taste at all like the food she was used to at home in America. She took her responsibilities as a mother very seriously. She wanted Florence to have nutritious meals, but she also wanted them to taste good.

The Nagels purchased their flour and sugar in one-hundred-pound bags in Canton because the local flour was so coarse that the bread made from it was almost impossible to eat. In spite of the fact that they stored the flour in large tins, the worms found it. Every few weeks, someone had to sift the flour and put it out in the sun to dry. The bugs also found the cereals. Even the rice was full of weevils. The Hakka people didn't mind the worms and weevils, but American palates couldn't accept them.

One day when Florence was four years old, she squatted beside their *amah* (helper) and watched intently while the *amah* sifted the flour and put all the worms carefully into a dish nearby.

"What are you keeping the worms for?" asked Florence in Chinese. Her blond curls bobbed up and down as she tried to see everything the *amah* was doing. Her little round face was lit with curiosity.

"Oh, little Lotus Blossom!" the *amah* said, her eyes sparkling. "Tonight I will make a delicious soup out of them for my family."

The Hakka ate only two meals a day, which made it nice for the women. They didn't need to cook during the heat of the day. Instead, everyone took a midday nap. The Nagels adopted both of these practices too.

Because the Hakkas were mostly farmers, their women had never bound their feet. These hard-working ladies did the same tasks the men did and wore the same type of clothes—loose slacks and a jacket with long sleeves and a high collar. There was a slight difference in style, though, between the men's and women's jackets. The men's jackets buttoned down the middle, but the women's jackets buttoned on the side. If they could afford it, men and women wore quilted jackets in the winter to keep out the cold. If they couldn't, they just wore all their summer clothes at the same time! Working women often had a baby strapped to their backs.

Time sped by quickly for the Nagels. Their neighbors, the Andersons, now had two little girls, Helen and Hazel. They were Florence's constant playmates.

And then it was almost furlough time. Four-and-a-half-year-old Florence waited eagerly for the much-anticipated day. At last she was going to meet the grandmothers and grandfathers she had never seen. Also, her mother had told her there was going to be a new baby in their own family!

Sherman was concerned about his wife having a baby so far from medical help. He decided the wisest course would be to send Florence and her mother home to America early. He planned to join them when it was officially furlough time.

So Mary was in America on May 26, 1915, when Florence's baby brother was born. Since she and her husband hadn't chosen

a name, she sent a cable to Wai Chow: SON BORN MAY 26 STOP WHAT IS HIS NAME STOP WE MISS YOU STOP GOD IS GOOD STOP MARY.

It took almost three months to receive a reply from Sherman telling her the baby would be called Sherman Albertus Nagel, Jr. By that time, the family was calling him Sonny—and the nickname stuck.

As exciting as it was to be in America, Florence was anxious to get back to Wai Chow. She had a little brother to show off to the Anderson girls next door. What

Sherman Albertus Nagel, Jr., known as Sonny, became Florence's little brother on May 26, 1915.

fun it would be to have a baby boy on the compound! First, however, she got to spend time with both sets of grandparents and meet all her aunts and uncles. And she had lots of cousins to play with.

People found it fascinating to hear Florence speak Chinese—a language she spoke more comfortably than English. When her father arrived in America on furlough, she visited many churches with her family, and her father spoke to the people about the needs of the mission work in China. Most of the people who came to hear him had never had the opportunity to meet real missionaries. They eagerly listened to the stories Pastor Nagel and his wife told.

Near the end of their furlough, the Nagels received a letter that saddened them. The Andersons wrote to say that they were accepting a call to the Swatow Mission. Another missionary family would be called to Wai Chow.

When the Nagel family boarded their ship for the return journey to China, a tall slender young couple introduced themselves as Albert and Julie Wearner. They were going to be the Nagels' new next-door neighbors. Florence was thrilled! They were such friendly people—and they had a baby boy, too!

Arriving on the compound at Wai Chow, the Nagels made quite a spectacle. Pastor Nagel had been unhappy with the chickens in China. They laid very few eggs, and the chickens themselves were small things. So he brought back American chickens—one dozen White Leghorns and one dozen Plymouth Rocks. They were beautiful chickens, and how the Chinese admired them! Before long, however, the chickens started disappearing one by one. It became a common sight to see the Nagels' chickens running all around the town and in nearby villages.

In Hong Kong, Florence's uncle Lee Nagel was keeping two beautiful Angora kittens for her. Sherman picked them up on one of his regular trips to that city. The kittens had been born on a British gunboat that already had its full quota of cats. So a sailor brought them to Uncle Lee's office.

How Florence loved those cats! One was gray, and one was brown. They became her constant playmates. Then one day the gray kitten was missing. The brown cat mourned and cried all day. He wouldn't eat for the next four days. By the fifth day, seven-year-old Florence was desperate. "Dear Jesus," she prayed, "please help me find my cat. Please, please bring him back to me."

During the night she had a strange dream. She saw her kitty coming home, walking on top of the wall in back of the house. The cat was thin and hungry, and oh, so dirty!

"Mother," Florence said the next morning at the breakfast table, "God is going to send my kitty home. I believe someone stole it to eat." Then she told the family about her dream. Suddenly she sat up straight, listening intently. "He's here!" she shouted, tearing out of the house. And there he was—just like in her dream. She hugged the scrawny, filthy cat, and bowed her head. "Thank You, Jesus," she said. "You brought my kitty home!"

This was the first of many times in her young life when Florence knew God heard and helped her. Each incident strengthened her faith in Him a little more.

About two years after the Nagels had returned to China from America, Pastor Nagel took the family to Hong Kong with him on one of his trips there. Florence was so excited! They stayed with Uncle Lee, who owned a fleet of fifteen small boats used to ferry passengers to and from the large ships anchored out in the bay. Whimsically, he named these boats *Walla Walla I, Walla Walla II, Walla Walla III,* and so forth. Many a Hong Kong tourist who had attended Walla Walla College was surprised and amused to see the name on these boats as they carried him to and from the ship. Inevitably, people made inquiries and later looked up Uncle Lee to renew an acquaintance or simply to swap stories about Walla Walla College.

Often Uncle Lee took his brother Sherman's family out for a ride on one of the boats. They would picnic along the coast, and the adults would thoroughly enjoy a day of relaxation and peace. The children, of course, were excited and happy.

On the last day of this particular vacation, Sherman went down to the office to tell his brother goodbye. As he turned to leave, an elderly American named Harry Detwilder stepped into the office.

Mr. Detwilder was a wealthy merchant from Los Angeles, traveling around the world with Mr. W. K. Kellogg of corn flakes fame. Mr. Kellogg had become extremely ill and was admitted to a hospital for a week or so of medical observation and treatment. Mr. Detwilder worried about his friend's illness, but he was also disappointed about missing his sightseeing time in China. How was he going to entertain himself for a whole week while Mr. Kellogg was in the hospital?

"If you really want to see China," Uncle Lee told him, pointing toward Sherman, "go with my brother here. He's heading home to Wai Chow. If you go with him, I guarantee you'll see all of China that you wish to see."

The details were soon arranged, and the next morning Mr. Detwilder eagerly met the Nagel family at the railroad station to begin the trip to Wai Chow. Little Florence immediately took to the small gray-haired man. She became his own special guide to her part of China. Whether riding on train or boat, she stayed beside him, telling him all about what he was seeing. For his part, he was delighted with the sparkling-eyed child who spoke Chinese as well as she did English. At each stop, he took her hand, and they walked together talking about the customs, the temples, or the people. And at just about every stop he bought some sort of pet for her. By the time the party reached Wai Chow, Florence had acquired two yellow canaries, a green parrot, two white mice, two fluffy bunnies, and a bag full of goldfish! Mr. Detwilder bought Florence and Sonny many new toys as well. They also had built a close bond of friendship.

CHAPTER THREE

Baggage, Bandits, and Battles

Part of Pastor Nagel's responsibilities as a missionary was to visit all the chapels and home churches in the Hakka Mission District and to encourage and advise the local Bible teacher in charge of each one. He also preached to the people and performed baptisms, marriages, and funerals. Whenever he left on one of these trips, he was absent from home for at least a month and sometimes as long as two months. Mother, Florence, and Sonny stayed at home waiting for him to return. These were lonely times—both for those who stayed and for the one who left.

"The next trip," Father announced one day, "I'm taking you all with me."

Florence bounced up and down. "Really, Papa? We can all go with you?"

"Really, Lotus Blossom," he replied with a smile. "But it will take lots of planning and work, so we'd better make a list of all the things that need to be done before we can leave."

Over the next few weeks, the Nagel house was a hive of activity. Mary baked extra loaves of bread. Then she sliced them and dried the slices in the oven until they were golden brown. Florence helped stack the slices in tin boxes and wrap the boxes in oiled paper. The toasted bread would keep fresh for weeks. Most of the time, they would eat whatever was available locally, but Mary wanted some emergency provisions.

Florence's schoolbooks had to go with them, of course. Mary was teaching Florence to read and do arithmetic.

Clothes for both the children and the adults needed to be packed. The children each chose a few small toys to take with them. Then there were folding cots and bedding. And mosquito nets were a must. They had to be hung over the beds each night to keep away the mosquitoes and other flying insects.

Dishes, cans of food, overshoes, umbrellas, coats—all were added to the growing pile of things that had to be packed in small bundles. Chinese porters would carry the bundles until they reached the river.

At last the day came! Very early on a Friday morning, everything was packed and ready to go. Father counted the bundles one last time, making a list of them. Mother was busy doing all the last-minute things that mothers everywhere do. Florence and Sonny were eagerly running up and down the steps, too excited to stand calmly and wait.

The porters chatted to each other as they made up the bundles each would carry. Four chair porters would carry each of the two sedan chairs that had been added to the amazing amount of things that needed to go on the trip. Florence and Sonny rode in one chair, and Mother in the other.

The men carried the covered chairs on long bamboo poles, and Florence and Sonny laughed as they bounced up and down. But by the time they reached their first stop at noon, they were glad to get out and walk on solid ground.

The Nagels stayed over Sabbath at the chapel nearest Wai Chow. The children watched mother make up beds for them on some boards placed over two sawhorses. The local teacher prepared supper. The children didn't mind eating native food, but their mother didn't like it very much. The next morning she went into the kitchen to prepare the breakfast herself.

Like good missionaries, Florence and Sonny stood at the chapel door to greet the people who came to worship. The worshipers were fascinated by the children. Even some people who were just passing by stopped to look. Few had ever seen white children before. Some of the braver ones reached out to touch Sonny's fair skin and his light hair. Then they ran off to tell their friends to come and see the little "foreign devils." Father invited them all to come in and join the meeting that was about to start. Out of curiosity, many of them came in—and listened.

The Nagel family stayed until Sunday morning at this first chapel. Then they packed up their things to start off again. This time they traveled only about a mile to the riverbank where the porters took off their burdens. A small boat waited to take the Nagels and their luggage to a steam launch waiting farther out in deeper water. By the time they actually got themselves and all of their supplies onto the steam launch, it was very late. Unfortunately, there was no room on the launch for them to sleep or even lie down on the floor. Father piled up the bundles and mother sat on them, holding Sonny on her lap so that he could sleep.

The following morning they disembarked at the next chapel on their itinerary. They were exhausted and sleepy. Unfortunately, the chapel was very small and very dirty. Flies covered everything.

Preparing to cross a river on one of Pastor Nagel's many trips throughout the interior of China as he visited the chapels and home churches in the Hakka Mission district.

Father and Mother sent the teacher to purchase a broom and mop. Then, with some water, they showed him how to clean up the place. The coconut husk broom and the rice straw mop may not have been up to modern standards, but they worked. Soon the meeting place looked clean and inviting.

After a stay of a few days, they left for another chapel farther up the river. This time they hired a cargo boat that was poled up the river by coolies. The night was calm and quiet. Peaceful. Suddenly from the riverbank a loud voice yelled out, "Halt! Pull over to the shore!"

Father knew that it must be bandits, and they dared not disobey. When the coolies pulled their boat to shore, the bandit chief held up a lantern to inspect the passengers. Father joined the boat's crew and explained that he was a missionary traveling with his family and visiting churches along the riverbank. While he talked, Mary prayed earnestly, asking God to protect her husband. And she pled with God to hide her children. She knew they could be taken hostage and held for ransom.

God softened the bandit chief's heart. "Just give me a little tea money," he said, "and I will let you continue this trip."

"Here," Pastor Nagel said. "Take this money. But I ask a favor in return. Tell me, are there other bands farther up the river?"

"Of course there are," the chief answered.

"Then, please, may I have a card from you?" Father asked as he prayed for guidance. "I can show it to the next band, and perhaps they will let us go free."

He got what he needed from the bandit chief, and the boat continued upriver. Several more times that night they were commanded to pull ashore, but the card from the first chief worked well. As soon as each bandit chief saw it, he let them go.

The northern part of the Hakka Mission territory was in famine. Many people had so little to eat that they went into the mountains to dig up the roots of trees. They dried the roots and ground them up and cooked them into a kind of porridge. Once a starving woman ran into the kitchen where Mother was cooking rice and snatched a handful of rice right out of the boiling water in the kettle!

Florence and Sonny got hungry too. Their own emergency food had been eaten. They had to depend on the extremely scarce local food.

"Mother," Florence complained one day, "I've eaten nothing but rice for fifteen days, and it just won't go down anymore."

"I'm sorry, dear," her mother said, "but we'll have to eat it a while longer. So we must be brave and not complain. Remember, we are doing it for Jesus, and He will help us eat it."

The day the Nagel family started out for Hin Nien, a drenching rain poured from the sky. They had forty miles to go that day over some very high mountains. The road was slippery, and the sedan-chair bearers could not keep their footing. Many times they slipped and almost fell. The sedan chairs leaked water, and the heavy wind threatened to topple them. Finally the porters told Mary and Florence they could carry them no longer. They had to get out of the chairs and walk. Sonny was so young and small he could ride, but not the others. They were still over twelve miles from their destination.

Just as they came over the last mountain, the sun broke through the clouds. They saw the most beautiful rainbow they had ever seen—made even more spectacular by the flaming sunset. It was as though God was assuring them of His wonderful promise to always be with them.

When they finally reached the chapel at Hin Nien, Florence and both her parents had big blisters on their feet. Pastor Nagel asked the teacher to boil a lot of water, and they all soaked their feet in it to relieve some of the pain so that they could sleep that night. They were so tired that even the board bed felt good.

After a few days, they left Hin Nien by boat to go to a village where they could catch the train into Swatow. On both banks of the river ahead of them warring factions were fighting each other. The boat captain would not risk his boat and passengers to go through the fighting, so he turned the boat around to go back upriver. Rather than go back, Pastor Nagel persuaded the crew of a large coal barge to take his family on board. The sleeping cots were set up right in the center of the boat. The coal all around them made a pretty good fortification. Two calm days passed.

On the third day, they heard the noise of gunfire in the distance.

Other boats were hurrying back up the river as fast as their crews could push them with their long poles. The men on these boats told the crew of the Nagels' barge about the serious battles ahead. Soldiers were commandeering every boat they could get their hands on. As rapidly as possible with a slow-moving barge, the captain sought a place of shelter. He finally found a huge rocky overhang around a bend in the river and anchored there. Sherman and Mary spent the time earnestly praying for the safety of their family.

The next day, they saw clouds of dust rising in the sky. Word came that it was formed by soldiers from the retreating army running for their lives. The Nagels didn't waste time trying to find another, faster boat. Pastor Nagel persuaded the crew to take this opportunity to slip quietly out of their hiding place and go down the river, past the armies.

They had traveled only a few hours downriver when they heard more fighting. All afternoon the big guns roared and echoed through the hills. There was nothing to do but find another shelter for the barge and wait—and pray.

Pastor Nagel read the ninety-first psalm and other comforting promises from his Bible. Once when the shooting was very near, Sonny became so frightened that he crawled under a cot. Mother heard him talking and leaned near to listen.

"Let not your heart be troubled," quoted Sonny, almost four years old. "If we trust God, we are safe anywhere."

The next morning, Sherman asked the crew to take him to a small village a mile or two ahead to buy some rice and eggs and vegetables. Before the barge reached the village, they saw soldiers on the other side of the river, running upstream as fast as they could go. As the boat went a little farther downstream, the captain and his crew looked for the other army, but there were no soldiers to be seen. They had run away, too. Later, they found out that on one side of the river the winning army had held its ground, but on the other side, the same army had lost. Confusion reigned everywhere.

As the crew guided the barge past the fighting area, Pastor Nagel gave thanks to the Lord. "This must be the Lord's doing," he said.

That was the last of the actual fighting they saw, but not the last of the soldiers.

CHAPTER FOUR

Deep Sadness, Deep Joy

Many soldiers, straggling behind the army, wanted the barge for their own transport in order to catch up to the others. Five times angry soldiers tried to take over the barge. But each time, when they saw the "white devils" on board, they left the barge as soon as possible. It took the Nagels three days to travel the last ninety miles to their destination.

When they reached the railroad, they found that so many people were fleeing from their homes, the trains were packed. People climbed on top of the trains; some even clung to the outside!

Conscious of his exhausted wife and children, Pastor Nagel pleaded with the conductor for a place on the next train for his family. Finally, some carefully hoarded silver coins secured them passage. Once they were on the train, it took only three hours to reach the port city of Swatow. The train depot was only a short distance from the mission compound, where they received an excited welcome from the Anderson family, their former next-door neighbors in Wai Chow.

The Nagels recuperated in Swatow, enjoying the kindness and friendship of the Andersons for a few days. The four children played happily together, and Florence thrilled the Anderson girls with stories of the wild adventures she and Sonny had just experienced.

Three days later, the Nagels boarded an ocean-going luxury liner for the overnight trip to Hong Kong. Florence wished the trip would last longer. It was such a beautiful ship—with good food and clean beds, and no guns or soldiers.

In the Hong Kong Harbor, one of Uncle Lee's Walla Walla boats met their ship. It had taken the family more than six weeks to visit all the Adventist chapels and negotiate their way through the battles to reach Hong Kong. When Pastor Nagel reported his trip to the mission headquarters, he found that he was the first Adventist missionary ever to take his family itinerating with him.

In Hong Kong, Mother stocked up on food supplies, and Father bought Bibles and tracts and books to take back for use in the mission.

The trip from Hong Kong to Wai Chow was simple and quick compared to the trip *to* Hong Kong. They took a train to Sheck Lung, then boarded a *to dai* for the trip up the East River. The next day Florence and Sonny saw the first glimpse of their city as they rounded the bend in the river.

Sonny squealed and ran in circles around his family. Florence grabbed the railing and leaned forward. "Oh, Mother," she said with a big smile, "isn't it good to be home again?"

Florence kept her eyes on the city as they drew near. Its walls, thirty feet high, and fifty feet thick at the base, were an impressive sight. The East River divided the city into east and west halves. And these mighty walls surrounded both halves of the city. Florence knew that the inside walls were terraced upward, leaving them just wide enough at the top for guards to march along them on patrol. Before long, their boat was sailing between the high walls of the east and west halves of Wai Chow. The Nagels were home at last!

★ ★ ★ ★ ★

For Florence, one of the highlights of her life in China came only every two years. These were the times when the family left the interior of China and went down to Canton to attend the South China Union meetings. These biennial meetings lasted for ten days. The Adventist missionaries, teachers, and Bible workers from all over Southern China met together—often bringing their families. The children got to play with other American children. They swam together, and sang, and heard thrilling new stories. It was as exciting as a ten-day picnic!

The summer when Florence was eight years old it was time for the South China Union meetings again. Florence and Sonny eagerly renewed friendships.

The president of the Far Eastern Division, I. H. Evans, spoke at the evening meetings. One day Florence heard some of the older children talking about him. "Elder Evans asked me to memorize a poem," one said. "He wanted me to recite it at the meeting tonight."

"Are you going to do it?" another asked.

"No," said the first speaker with a shrug of his shoulders. "I can't memorize that fast. Besides, I don't want to do it."

A third piped up, "He asked me, too. But I told him I had to watch my baby brother during the meeting, so I couldn't do it."

The others laughed.

Florence listened in wonder. *How can they say No to the man in charge of all the churches in Southern China?* she asked herself. *Aren't they afraid to say No? They must be brave!*

It was early afternoon when Elder Evans stopped Florence outside the meeting tent. "Florence, I wonder if you could do me a favor," he began.

Florence felt her heart sink. But she stood politely, waiting for him to continue.

"During my sermon this evening, I have a poem I'd like you to recite to the congregation. Would you do that for me?"

Florence stammered, trying to figure out what to say. Then she remembered what she'd heard from the older children. Could she say No, too? It was worth a try. She stood up a little taller.

"I'm sorry, sir," she said. "I can't do it tonight." The disappointed look on his face went straight to her heart, but she soon ran off to play with friends and forgot about it.

About an hour later, four-year-old Sonny called her. "Papa says to come right now," he said.

"Why?"

"I don't know," he shrugged.

When Florence arrived in the room crowded with bedrolls, clothes, and books, Father was waiting. He put a hand on her shoulder and looked silently down into her eyes for a long moment.

Then he took a deep breath and spoke firmly. "No girl of mine ever says No when she is asked to do something for the Lord," he said.

"But, Father!" Florence whined. "The meeting begins in three hours. I can't learn a poem that fast." Then she remembered what she'd heard that afternoon and lifted her chin. She looked him straight in the eye and said, "I won't do it."

A sad, almost defeated look came over her father's face. But he took her by the arm, saying, "Oh, yes, you will."

What followed was something Florence later preferred to forget. It was the last spanking she ever received from her father.

When meeting time came, little Florence walked onto the platform with the ministers and sat down beside Elder Evans. She recited the poem in front of two hundred people without a mistake. And while Elder Evans spoke to the congregation, Florence thought about the spanking she'd received that afternoon. She knew she was wrong to have spoken to Father as she had; she knew she deserved her punishment. And she knew the older children she had listened to were wrong. A warm feeling of pleasure filled her spirit. She felt so good now that she had recited the poem.

After the meeting, Elder Evans thanked her, and they continued to talk for a while. In the ensuing years, he and his wife wrote to Florence every few months, encouraging her to stay close to the Lord and urging her to prepare her life for foreign mission service when she grew older. They tried to help her realize that real happiness is found only when a person says Yes to God.

Ezra and Inez Longway, young missionaries on their way to Siam, also attended the South China Union meetings. They became popular with the children, joining in their games and marveling at their fluency in the languages of their home territories.

★ ★ ★ ★ ★

About a year later, Pastor Nagel received a letter from their former Wai Chow neighbor, Pastor Anderson. Father gathered his family around him to share the letter. Pastor Anderson wrote that his wife, Helen and Hazel's mother, had passed away. He was lost without his dear wife, but he felt that the Lord wanted him to stay in Asia.

Father paused and blew his nose. Mother patted his arm and wiped tears from her cheeks. Finally Father continued reading.

The letter went on to say that Pastor Anderson had been asked to go with a colporteur by the name of Tan Kia O to look over French Indo-China and see what the possibility was for opening up a mission there.

"Now, dear friends," the letter went on, "here is the crux of the matter. Would you be willing to make a home for my little girls? They need a mother's care so badly right now while I travel. It will be for only two years, I hope."

"Really, Father? Really? Can they come?" Florence asked. Her excitement conflicted with her sadness for poor Mrs. Anderson.

Mother smiled through her tears. "Of course, they can come. That poor man! This is one worry we can help him with. Sherman, write and tell him to bring the girls here. We'll take care of them. We have plenty of room."

Little missionaries on the Wai Chow compound. From left to right: Robert Wearner, Sonny, Florence, Audry Wearner, Helen Anderson, and Hazel Anderson.

It had been more than four years since the Andersons had lived next door. And in spite of the sad loss of their mother, Helen and Hazel were glad to be back with their friends—almost as glad as Florence and Sonny were to have them back.

Soon Pastor Anderson was writing letters, telling them all about the interesting things he was seeing. He sent them pictures of the newly discovered Angkor Wat in Cambodia, the largest religious monument in the world. Its ancient ruins were being repaired for future visitors to see.

When Pastor Anderson brought his girls to Wai Chow to stay with the Nagels, he brought all the family's personal belongings, including his library of more than a thousand books. This library opened up a whole new world to Florence. Almost every evening after worship she read aloud by the light of the kerosene lamp. The other children lay on the floor beside her, listening.

As the weeks went by, she read the biographies of great missionaries such as Livingstone of Africa, Carey of India, Judson of Burma, and Taylor of China. The children even enjoyed history books such as Wylie's *History of the Reformation* and Abbott's *Histories of European Monarchs*. Before the two years were over, Florence had read every Primary, Junior, and many Senior Reading Course books.* She read them for every year since the Reading Course lists had begun. The *National Geographic Magazine* arrived monthly as well as *The Youth's Instructor* and *Our Little Friend*. In this way, the children learned a lot about the rest of the world, even though the area where they lived was remote and unknown by most of the world.

These two years were especially busy ones for Mary Nagel. In addition to having a school at home for the four children, she opened a girls' school in the city. This took much supervision and planning. Mary received instructions about how and what to teach from the Fireside Correspondence School in Washington, D.C.**

When Father was at home, he met with Florence every morning for several hours to hear her recite her lessons. Later Florence relied totally on the correspondence course. She completed sixth grade through her first year of college with the Fireside Correspondence School.

Soon after Mary started the girls' school, it became clear that she needed extra help at home to do the washing and cleaning. So

*For many years, the Youth Department of the church produced a list of recommended reading for different age levels.

**Now called Home Study International.

a lovely Chinese Christian family came to work for the Nagels. Chung Ah Vu became the gateman and did all of the buying for the compound. He also supervised the compound gardeners. Following Mary's instructions, he soon had the place looking like a beautiful park; tropical flowers blossomed all over the compound.

His wife, Chung Ah Tien, washed clothes and cleaned the Nagels' home. But more importantly, she helped with the cooking, and she supervised the children while Mother was in town at the girls' school. The Chungs had two children of their own who became playmates for the missionaries' children. Their son Ah Tsao was eight years old, and their daughter Tshi Oi was seven. Three more daughters were born to the Chungs in the next few years. These children soon became like brother and sisters to the American children. (Years later, all the Chung daughters graduated with degrees in nursing, and several worked in mission hospitals in Asia.)

In addition to the biennial meetings in Canton, yearly meetings were held for the workers of the Hakka Mission. All the pastors and Bible workers came to the Wai Chow compound. As the meetings were about to begin in the fall of 1920, the air was filled with excitement. Meade McGuire from the General Conference of Seventh-day Adventists in Washington, D.C., was to be the guest speaker! And several other speakers were coming from the Division office. That was exciting enough. But Mary Nagel looked forward with real eagerness to the arrival of R. M. Milne from the Union office in Hong Kong because he was bringing his wife! No American woman had ever accompanied her visiting husband to these meetings before. But Mrs. Milne was actually coming! Pastor and Mrs. Milne had just arrived in China during the summer of 1920. He was the publishing director of the South China Union.

Alma Milne was a bubbly young woman, filled with energy and interested in everything around her. She told fascinating stories to the children; she seemed to love the children almost as much as she loved Jesus. Florence Nagel thought Mrs. Milne was the most beautiful lady she'd ever seen. She determined to grow up to be just like her. How special this meeting time was to Florence! Even Elder McGuire, the guest speaker, spent a couple of hours every day with the children. He took them on long walks, and he talked with them

In the fall of 1920, general meetings were held at Wai Chow for the workers in the Hakka Mission district. During these meetings, Florence decided to be baptized. Pastor and Mrs. Nagel are seated in the front row—second and sixth from the left, respectively.

about Jesus—and he listened to them talk about their own concerns. As Florence studied his face, she was convinced that Jesus must have looked a lot like Elder McGuire.

The only dark spot during the meetings came when Chung Ah Vu came to the house one evening looking for Pastor Nagel.

"He's not here just now," Mother said. "Can I help you?"

Ah Vu looked disconcerted. "Uh . . . I . . . um . . ." He swallowed. "I think I need to see Pastor Nagel right away," he finally blurted out.

Mother told him where to find her husband, so he ran off in that direction. Within minutes, Father came into the living room calling for the family.

"What is it, Sherman?" Mary asked as she hurried in. "You look serious."

"I am serious," he said. He looked at the children as they entered. "Good. Thank you for coming so quickly. We have to talk." He held up a crumpled piece of paper. "This was wrapped around a rock and hurled at Ah Vu this evening." He smoothed the small note in his hand, while Florence held her breath.

Father looked again at the Chinese characters on the paper. "It's addressed," he continued, "to the 'brown-haired missionary with the little boy.' " Mother gasped, and Florence's eyes opened wide. Sonny grinned. Helen and Hazel sat silent and wide-eyed.

"Here is what it says as near as I can make out," Father went on. "The handwriting is very poor. 'We get your boy, white devil missionary. We get him soon.' " Father returned the note to his pocket and sat down.

"Papa, what shall we do?" Florence asked. After all, she was ten years old and felt some responsibility for her little brother.

"First of all, we'll pray. Then we'll move your bed, Sonny, into our bedroom. I think you'll be pretty safe during the daylight hours. But just in case, we'll all be watchful. Report any stranger on the compound to the nearest adult. And, Sonny," Father said, looking right at him, "don't take any chances. And don't leave the compound."

Sonny opened his mouth to protest, but Father stopped him. "Yes, I know that you sometimes slip out to go play by the river. Don't do it now. Be really careful, son."

"Yes, Father," Sonny replied, wrinkling his nose. "But how did you know I went to the river?"

Father smiled and said, "You'd be surprised."

The week sped by, and soon the last weekend of the meetings came. On Friday morning, there were so many people to prepare meals for and such a lot of work to do to get everyone ready for the Sabbath that Mother and Ah Tien were almost frantic. Mother allowed Helen and Florence to go to the morning devotional service to hear Elder McGuire speak, calling after them to hurry home to help as soon as the meeting was over. Hazel and Sonny were out in the playhouse with Ah Tien's children. Mother had given the children special instructions not to pick any of the roses. She wanted them for a beautiful bouquet in the church for the Sabbath services the next day.

After the meeting Helen returned right away, but Florence did not. She wandered home about a half hour later.

"Why are you so late?" demanded Mother.

Florence had a faraway look in her eye. "Oh, Mother!" she replied. "You should have been there. Elder McGuire gave such an appealing sermon this morning. And right after that Pastor Anderson asked if anyone wished to be baptized. Then he wanted to meet with us after the meeting." She paused.

"And, Mother," she said in a rush, "Lucy, Giang Lan, and I are all going to be baptized tomorrow! I'm so very happy, Mother."

"Praise the Lord!" Mother said, giving Florence a hug. "Your father and I have been praying for this." Then she turned back to the stove, saying, "But for now, let's finish getting ready for Sabbath and all the company. Florence, bring me a dozen eggs. Helen, chop these carrots now, please."

Several hours later Mother stopped abruptly. "Where are Sonny and Hazel? I got so busy I forgot about them. Florence, hurry and go see what they are up to. They were in the playhouse with Ah Tien's children last time I checked."

Florence returned within minutes, panting for breath. "Mother, I can't find them! Ah Tien's children are at the gate with their father. They don't know where Sonny and Hazel are. Oh, Mother! Do you think they've been kidnapped? Do you, Mother?"

Mother's face turned pale. She clutched the table, then sat down suddenly.

"Florence, go to the church quickly and get your father!" she ordered.

Florence ran across the compound to the church. Once she located Father among the congregation, she had to get his attention—without attracting too much attention herself. Finally she caught his eye and motioned him to come.

When he reached her, she pulled him outside. "Father! Sonny and Hazel are missing! We can't find them anywhere!"

He looked at Florence for an instant. She was sure he was remembering the threatening note. Suddenly, he turned on his heel and quickly reentered the church. Florence ran after him, wondering why he didn't come home.

From the back of the church, he spoke in a loud voice, "Brethren, I'm sorry to interrupt this meeting. But my son and little Hazel Anderson are missing. Bandits have threatened to kidnap him, and I'm worried. Please, will you help find the children? And, please, pray!"

The meeting was dismissed immediately; everyone set out to look for the missing children. The police were notified and joined in the search. The men searched all the neighboring villages, but they could find no trace of either child. Two hours passed. No Sonny. No Hazel.

CHAPTER FIVE

Another Furlough

Back at the Nagel home, Mother was weeping and wringing her hands.

"Oh, Mrs. Nagel," Ah Tien said, taking her by the arm. "Come, let us look once more among the boxes stored in the basement. Perhaps we missed something the first time."

As they searched, Mother continued to sob and pray.

Then a little five-year-old voice asked, "Mother? Why are you crying?"

"Sonny!" she shrieked. And that was all she could say. Tears streamed down her face as she hugged her son as though she'd never let him go. Ah Tien stood next to her, patting Sonny's back.

Finally Mother brushed his hair out of his eyes and said, "Thank God you are alive, Sonny! I thought bandits had stolen you."

Sonny snuggled into her lap. "I'm sorry, Mother. I didn't mean to scare you. We thought you'd be mad at us so we hided."

Mother squeezed him. Then she lifted her head abruptly.

"Where is Hazel?" she asked. "Is she down here too?"

Sonny silently pointed to a pile of empty boxes in the far corner.

Ah Tien raced to them and began pulling boxes down and looking inside. Then she stopped and smiled. A moment later, she lifted the sleeping Hazel from her hiding place.

Up in the living room sometime later, after messengers had been sent to tell the searchers that the lost children were found, Sonny and Hazel told about their afternoon. There had been a wedding on the compound during the week, and in true childhood fashion, they decided to play wedding. "And a bride has to have flowers, you know," Sonny explained, avoiding his mother's eyes. "So we picked a rose. We knew you wouldn't miss one rose. It was so pretty, Mother. But it looked so little. So we picked another one. We didn't think you'd notice."

Sonny gulped before he continued bravely. "We just kept picking . . . and . . . and . . . pretty soon we had a nice, big bouquet. It was so pretty. And all of a sudden the roses were all gone . . . the bushes were empty!"

Mother's mouth settled into a firm line as she listened.

"Then we remembered you told us not to pick them," Sonny said. "And we guessed you'd be mad. But a bride needs lots of flowers, doesn't she? And we didn't want to get in trouble, so we got in the boxes and hoped you wouldn't see that the flowers were all gone."

Mother took a deep breath. "You knew I wanted the roses for church. I told you not to pick them, but you did. I'm very disappointed in you both. Then you hid—just like Adam and Eve did in the Garden of Eden. And now you're making excuses." Mother took a deep breath before she continued. "Because you disobeyed, there will be no roses in church tomorrow."

Sonny and Hazel looked at their shoe tops. Finally Sonny muttered, "We're sorry, Mother. We really are."

Mother stood up. "I'm sure you are," she said. "Now come upstairs to my bedroom. You're going to be a little more sorry."

Sonny and Hazel silently followed Mother up the stairs.

The next morning Mother called Florence and Helen early to help her get breakfast for the guests. The day had dawned chilly and overcast, and it looked like it could rain any minute. But Florence's heart was filled with happiness. Today, her brother was home—he had not been kidnapped. And today she would be baptized and become a member of the church just like the grown-ups. She knew she loved Jesus, and she wanted to grow up to be a missionary—just like her parents.

Elder McGuire gave a wonderful sermon that morning, and at the end, he invited everyone to go down to the river for the baptism. Just as all the baptismal candidates came to the riverbank, the black clouds separated, and the sun sparkled through! Pastor Anderson, Helen and Hazel's father, stepped down into the river and baptized the men and boys first. Then one by one, the three girls were baptized. It was Christmas Day, 1920.

The black clouds closed in as Pastor Anderson began praying—in three languages: Hakka, Cantonese, and English. The sunshine completely disappeared, and a cold wind began to blow. The wet, newly baptized people hurried to change into dry clothes. Before they reached shelter, however, the skies opened up, releasing a torrent of rain. But nothing could dampen Florence's spirits. She belonged to God now; she was His girl!

★ ★ ★ ★ ★

Shortly after Florence's twelfth birthday, Pastor Anderson came and took Helen and Hazel. He wasn't traveling so much now, and he missed his daughters. For Florence and Sonny this was a sad time. Helen and Hazel had become like their own sisters.

There was another reason Helen and Hazel needed to leave—their health. For several months, Florence had been in bed with malaria. Then she got dengue fever. The dengue fever was known locally as "break bone fever" because a person lost strength in the legs, and the bones just seemed to fold under when any pressure was put on them. Oh, how her legs ached! When she looked in the mirror, she noticed that her skin had a yellow tint—and it itched, too.

Recovery was a slow process. Florence finally graduated from the bed to a big chair where she huddled, trying to read a book. She was getting better, but she was still too weak to be concerned with the bustle of activity that was going on around her. For while Florence was recovering, the Nagel family was busily preparing for furlough again.

At last, Florence's condition seemed to be stabilizing, but could she make the long trip? The doctor finally said she could go. So

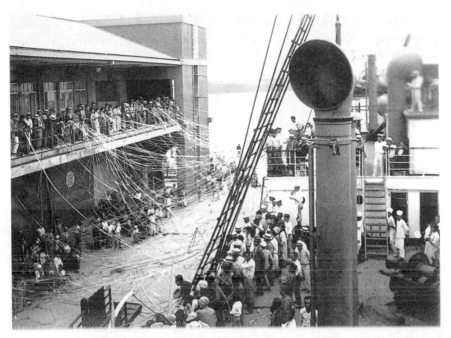

In 1922, the Nagels sailed from China on furlough to Canada and the U.S. aboard the Empress of Russia.

when the time came, the Nagels boarded the *Empress of Russia*, a luxury liner that could make the ocean crossing in only three weeks. This time they would be landing in Canada.

Everything went smoothly on the journey—until the ship docked. When the Nagels reached the front of the long line making its way past the immigration booths, they discovered that they faced an unforeseen problem. The Canadian immigration officer checked the family's passports against his list, then he glanced up at them and read the list again.

"Where did you pick up this little girl?" the official asked, looking at Florence. "Only three Nagels are on this list of American passengers."

Father nervously cleared his throat before he answered. "She is my daughter," he said. "She was born in Macau, but this isn't her first trip to North America. We've never had a problem getting her in before. Perhaps she is on the Portuguese passenger list."

While the officer looked for that list, Father turned to Florence. "I guess you'll have to go back to China, Lotus Blossom," he said. His forehead was furrowed, but his eyes still twinkled at her. "They don't seem to want you here."

It took quite a while to get things straightened out. When they finally were cleared by immigration, they entered the beautiful, cold sunshine of a Canadian winter.

Father and Mother were still concerned about Florence, so before they proceeded on their trip, Father arranged for his family to go across the channel to Victoria. An old classmate of his was the medical director of Rest Haven Sanitarium, a Seventh-day Adventist health-care institution. Situated on a small peninsula just where the bay enters the Pacific Ocean., it lay among pine trees and was designed to give city dwellers a place to renew their health and their spirits.

After a few weeks at Rest Haven, Florence began regaining some of the strength and weight she had lost. She became so much better that the Nagels went back to Vancouver and boarded a train that took them through the Canadian Rockies to Lacombe, Alberta. Florence and Sonny exclaimed about the speed of the train. It was much faster than the little train they rode in China. How much fun it was to go to sleep in a real bed on the train, and let the clickety-clack of the train wheels on the rails lull them to sleep that night!

The next morning brought a surprise. Sonny woke up early and grew restless as the rest of the family continued sleeping. He pulled up the window covering just a tiny bit and peeked out. Suddenly he looked again. Then he pushed the shade clear up and stared again out the window.

"Papa!" he yelled. "Look!"

Father rolled over and looked at him. "What's the matter, Sonny?"

"Look outside!" Sonny said. "What happened? Where did the green go? Everything is white!"

Father sat up and smiled. Then he reached over to wake up Florence. "Look outside," he told her. "Get your first glimpse of snow."

The snow had turned the mountains into a fairyland. The trees, the bushes, even the craggy boulders near the tracks were covered with a beautiful layer of crisp white snow.

When the train reached the Lacombe station, most of the snow had been left behind—but not the memory of it. On the train platform, Father pointed out his sister, Aunt Iva, and her husband, Ernest Hanson, who taught at Lacombe Junior College, now called Canadian University College.

Sonny ran up to them, shouting, "I saw snow! It was white and covered everything. It was so pretty!"

They laughed as they hugged and kissed the Nagels. "Stay here with us for a while," Aunt Iva said, "and you'll see more snow than you could wish for."

For a month the Nagel family stayed with the Hansons. Pastor Nagel conducted a Week of Prayer at the junior college and spent some time in the library studying. But it was so cold that the children were afraid to go outside. Another problem was the food. It was completely different from what Sonny and Florence ate at home in Wai Chow. Over the next three or four months, Florence once again started losing weight and growing lethargic. Her parents took her to a doctor again.

"She was getting stronger until we got here," Mother told the doctor. "Now she seems to be fading away. I'm really worried."

The doctor checked Florence carefully and asked her questions. He listened to her answers. Finally he was ready to talk to her parents.

"There's nothing really wrong with your daughter," he told them. "She's just cold and hungry."

Florence's parents looked startled, but the doctor continued. "Take her to a warmer climate," he said. "And get her some food that she's used to. Some rice, for instance, and whatever else she eats in China. She'll recover just fine."

"We had intended to go next to San Francisco for the General Conference session," Father replied. "So we'll just go sooner than we planned and visit her grandparents. That should take care of things for her."

San Francisco reminded Florence of Hong Kong—except it was not as beautiful, she thought. But a visit to downtown Chinatown made her feel much more at home. And how delicious the food tasted!

After the General Conference session ended, the Nagels traveled south to Mountain View, California, the home of Pacific Press Publishing Association. Many of the books Florence had read out loud in Wai Chow were printed here. She was fascinated with the big presses that were printing an issue of *Our Little Friend*. The real thrill, however, came when Father led her and Sonny into a big room where new books were displayed.

"Look at these books," he said, "and pick out the ones you would like to have. We will buy them and have them sent to Wai Chow right away, so they'll be there when we get home."

How exciting! Florence spent the next several hours happily poring over the books and making selections. She prayed while she fingered each book. After all, she was God's girl now, and He knew what she needed to learn so she could be a missionary herself someday.

The Canadian doctor's diagnosis of Florence had indeed been correct. In the last eleven months of the furlough, she grew nine inches and added thirty pounds! By the last month, she was eager to go home. She was homesick for Wai Chow and her friends.

On Thanksgiving Day the Nagels boarded their ship and sailed out of San Francisco Bay, bound for China. The first port of call was Manila. This was considerably off the direct route to Hong Kong, so they wouldn't reach home until after New Year's Day.

Three days before they reached Hong Kong, Father received a telegram. Florence watched his face anxiously, trying to see if it was good news or bad news. When he finished reading it he folded it and stuffed it in his shirt pocket—instead of reading it out loud to the family.

"Papa? What is it?" Florence asked. "Is it bad news?"

"No," he answered slowly. "I don't think so."

Then Florence saw the twinkle in his eyes.

"Tell us, Papa," she begged.

"Oh, you'll find out soon enough," he said.

"When?"

"As soon as we get home." And not another word would he say about it.

CHAPTER SIX

Gunboats and Hard Times

When they reached home, Florence was delighted to find Helen and Hazel Anderson waiting for them at the gate. And there was another surprise—a new face on the compound. This was what Father's telegram had been about!

Miss Ethel Edwards had worked in the General Conference office in Washington, D.C., for more than twenty years. She and Pastor Anderson had become acquainted through mutual friends. Letters followed, but they had never met in person. Then like the story of Rebekah in the Bible, Ethel traveled to Shanghai to marry J. P. Anderson and on to Wai Chow to be mother to his daughters. The Wearners had moved to Shanghai while the Nagels were on furlough, and Pastor Anderson and his family had moved back into the house next door. Florence was ecstatic!

The new Mrs. Anderson was a charming, talented lady. She could play the piano and sing beautifully. She was also a good cook. Before long she won the hearts of the children with all the special treats she made in her kitchen.

The next time Pastor Nagel went down to Hong Kong, he bought a lovely piano. Florence was thrilled because, after all, if she was going to be a missionary when she grew up, it would be helpful to be able to play the piano, wouldn't it? So she willingly took piano lessons from Mrs. Anderson.

Mrs. Anderson also organized the four children into a chorus and taught them many songs. Whenever their fathers would return from trips, the children entertained them with music, poems, and readings. Life on the compound was definitely livelier since the new Mrs. Anderson had arrived.

With no telephones, radio, or even a phonograph, the adults were virtually cut off from the world they once knew. The children, however, didn't feel deprived at all. They looked forward to the weekends—especially when their fathers were not traveling. On Friday and Sabbath evenings they had sundown worship together, meeting in alternate homes each week. After the children sang their favorite songs around the piano, one of the fathers would tell an exciting story from his travels or report on an article he had read. But it was the Bible quizzes Florence enjoyed the most. The quizzes sharpened her already keen interest in learning more about the Bible and the people in it.

Almost every Saturday evening was declared "Compound Night." The parents played games with the children. The mothers produced special treats they had made and kept hidden until game time. These were special times for the families. And so were birthdays, anniversaries, and holidays—both American and Chinese. The families on the compound celebrated everything together. In fact they even made up a few holidays to celebrate—days like "Everybody Wear Green Day" or "Sonny Lost a Tooth Day!" Everyone—adults as well as children—enjoyed these days.

Life on the compound also had a more serious side. When she was ten, Florence began teaching a kindergarten class in Sabbath School every week. By the time she was twelve, she was teaching a Bible class at the girls' school in town. She felt she was already beginning her mission service. She spent time with her Bible every day and prayed that God would prepare her for life as a grown-up missionary. A deep commitment to God's work in China was growing inside her.

Not long after the Nagels returned from their furlough, it was time once again for the biennial meetings of the South China Union Mission workers at Amoy. About halfway through the ten days of meetings, some large naval ships sailed into the bay, and soon the sounds of guns and cannons echoed from the opposite side of the water. Many of the older boys, along with Florence and a few adults, climbed the hill to the cemetery near the school and peeked out from behind the tombs to watch the battle.

Florence looked up at a man crouching beside her and commented, "This sounds like home." The sound of guns had become common in her life over the last few years.

As the political unrest grew in and around Amoy, the United States Embassy became concerned about the large number of Americans gathered on the island. So the embassy commissioned the USS *Asheville* to go to Kulangshu. The 240-foot gunboat anchored right out in front of the school for the remainder of the meetings.

When they were off duty, some of the sailors joined the missionaries as they swam in the bay. A few even attended the evening meetings. Because of the friendship of the missionaries and the inspiring meetings, one sailor committed his life to God. Later when he was discharged from the navy, he went home to the United States and enrolled in Union College.

After the meetings ended, the Nagel family visited Mother's brother, Victor M. Hansen, and his wife, Letha, on the mission compound in Canton. Their visit stretched out much longer than they had intended; fighting broke out again on the East River making it dangerous to try to go home. It was rumored that Dr. Sun Yat-sen was dying of cancer. General Chiang Kai-shek and the Nationalist Army tried to unite the country and maintain some control over the powerful warlords and their private armies. Day after day orders from the American Embassy read: NO TRAVELING INTO THE INTERIOR OF CHINA IS PERMITTED.

In Canton, Alma Milne conducted a summer school for teachers of the mission schools. Although she was only thirteen years old, Florence was allowed to enroll in some of the classes. She didn't plan to be a teacher, but she enjoyed the classes immensely.

September came, and Mrs. Milne organized a school for the missionary children—both those who lived there and those who were stranded there unable to go home. For the first time in her life, Florence was actually going to a school instead of studying her lessons by correspondence. And she had a classmate—Leland

Parker—in her own grade. Mrs. Milne was a charming teacher, and how Florence did love her! School was so much more fun than doing lessons by correspondence. Florence knew, however, that her time in the school might be cut short because her father was anxious to get back to Wai Chow.

Indeed Pastor Nagel had been inquiring about the possibility of traveling to Wai Chow by a back road that he hoped would bypass the fighting. He decided to go by himself first to see if he could get through and to find out what was happening at home. His family could stay safely in Canton a little longer. In spite of the edict from the American Embassy, Pastor Nagel arranged with a hostler to meet him with some horses at a nearby village in two days.

The morning he was going to slip away to meet the hostler, Pastor Nagel felt a sharp pain in his abdomen. It cramped him so badly that he didn't dare leave. By evening the pain was unbearable. His wife rushed him to the hospital. Unfortunately, the pain was so general that the doctors couldn't locate the cause. So they gave him sedatives and kept him under observation. Mary stayed with him during the day, feeding him, wiping the perspiration from his face, and making him as comfortable as she could. A friend, named Lyle Wilcox, stayed with him at night.

The first night Father was in the hospital, Aunt Letha was also rushed to the hospital. And before morning a new cousin was born, Victor Hansen, Jr. Another woman who also lived on the compound, Mrs. Harry Parker, was also admitted to the hospital. She was later diagnosed with typhoid fever and remained in the hospital for more than six weeks. For a while, it seemed that most of the adults on the compound were either sick or attending the sick.

Father had been in the hospital for two days when a battle broke out right in Canton. The fighting started in the streets surrounding the compound. Once Florence looked out the window for just a few moments—and a bullet came zinging through the air and hit the window casing beside her. Needless to say, though the battle raged just outside, no one looked out at the fighting anymore.

Then the battle spread into the town; it was especially heavy around the hospital. The patients were put on mattresses on the floor for safety. Father sat up against a wall so he would not be in danger from stray bullets. Suddenly he felt a stabbing pain in his lower right abdomen. Then—just as suddenly—he began to feel better. Jokingly he remarked, "All it takes to get me well is one good battle."

The next day was a different story. He doubled over and groaned in pain. He hurt so badly, he asked God to either take away the pain or let him die. Finally a doctor realized that the severe pain he had experienced the day before had been caused by his appendix rupturing. Pastor Nagel was immediately rushed into surgery. He underwent a total of three operations over the next several days, but still the infection continued draining. His weight dropped from 150 pounds down to a dangerously thin 100 pounds. In fact, the doctor gave up all hope for his recovery.

The missionaries and church members prayed earnestly, begging God to let him live. They even gathered around his bed to pray and anoint him. They wanted him to be healed; they needed him. But they managed to pray those difficult words, "Thy will be done." God heard their prayers, and Pastor Nagel began a slow recovery. Later, the Buddhist doctor remarked that his recovery was made possible through the will of God—and because the patient didn't smoke or drink or eat meat. Still, it was weeks before Pastor Nagel could even begin making plans to return to Wai Chow.

This was a hard time on the Canton compound—for the adults. Meanwhile, the children were enthusiastically planning a Christmas program with Mrs. Milne. Florence and Sonny had never seen or been involved in a Christmas program, so this was an exciting time for them. Even after her father became well enough to travel to Wai Chow, Florence was so engrossed in their plans for a wonderful program that she hardly missed him when he left. The program would take place two days before Christmas. She and Sonny looked forward to being with the large mission family over the holidays.

Then four days before the long-anticipated Christmas program, Father returned to Canton. "The political situation has cleared somewhat" he said. "So I want to take you all home with me. We'll leave early tomorrow morning!"

CHAPTER SEVEN

Refugees in the Basement

Florence swallowed a lump in her throat. *They couldn't leave now—not before the Christmas program!*

Mother interrupted her thought. "What happened to the Andersons?" she asked. "Did they stay up there in Wai Chow?"

"Yes, they did," Father said with a chuckle. "All this scare about going back! The Andersons have been there all along—and they haven't seen any fighting at all!"

Florence slipped out of the room. She needed to find a quiet place to be alone. Tears streamed down her face, and her heart felt like it was breaking. Her very first Christmas program—and she was going to miss it!

Florence kept remembering that she was God's girl now, but she still keenly felt the loss of the Christmas program. After the Nagels returned to Wai Chow, Mrs. Anderson overheard Florence explaining to Helen and Hazel all about the wonderful program she was missing.

"Why don't we give the program here?" Mrs. Anderson asked. "Florence, you can teach the songs and poems to Helen and Hazel, and the four of you can do the program for us. How about it?"

The girls jumped up and down, squealing happily. Then they found Sonny and told him the wonderful news. Florence and Sonny got busy teaching the poems and songs to Helen and Hazel. Mrs.

Anderson asked the gateman to find a small tree. And both mothers began making Christmas cookies and candies with fruit and nuts.

The children had never decorated a Christmas tree before, so Mrs. Anderson helped them make paper chains and popcorn ropes. Florence was delighted with the tree. Before the day was over, gifts mysteriously appeared under it. On Christmas Day, the program went off without a hitch, and the two families spent an unforgettable holiday together.

★ ★ ★ ★ ★

"Oh, no! Not again!" Florence gasped. She was fourteen now—and tired of war. She listened while one of the workers from the chapel nearby told Father that the army was heading for Wai Chow.

The Chinese revolutionary leader Dr. Sun Yat-sen had died in March, and now the Nationalist Army was completely under the leadership of General Chiang Kai-shek. It was on its way now, preparing to surround the city. The army moved into the narrow strip of land between the two rivers, near the compound. For a number of weeks, the army had never been far from the city, but it camped in the area near the compound only when it was either trying to starve the city into surrendering or had some new method of attack.

Wai Chow, China. Frequently during the years of revolutionary struggle in China, fighting came to this city where the Adventist mission compound was located. General Chiang Kai-shek, leader of the Nationalist Army, placed his cannons on the mountains across the river in the far distance of this photo and on the hills to the left.

51

General Chiang's frequent invasions of Wai Chow had lasted for more than three years now. Every few months, his army reorganized and came to try once more to capture the city. The city would get help from some robber bands up in the mountains and drive the army away. Many of these outlaw bands had belonged to the old warlords. Each warlord ruled over a certain district. But now General Yong Kwuen Ye was the district magistrate at Wai Chow. At each invasion, his forces had prevented General Chiang's soldiers from taking over the city.

General Yong was friendly toward the missionaries in Wai Chow. The Nagels and Andersons were the only American Seventh-day Adventist workers in this part of the interior of China. If they fled every time the attacking armies came, they would not be able to carry on any mission work at all. In fact, Pastor Nagel was so well known that the soldiers on outpost duty gave him a pass to come and go as he needed. Sometimes, they even sent a few soldiers with him, wherever he wished to go, to ensure his safety.

One time he returned from a trip absolutely exhausted.

"What happened, Papa?" Florence asked.

"Bandits happened, my dear," he said. Then he sat up straight. "And so did God's power! Would you like to hear how strong God is?"

"Oh, yes," Florence answered, barely breathing. "What happened?"

Father leaned back into his big chair and began his story as Sonny slipped into the room and settled on the floor near him.

"Do you remember that little chapel about twenty miles from here? Well, three days ago bandits stole most of the supplies from the school there. And then they robbed the pastor's home. They just go where they please and take anything they want.

"I didn't intend to let those bandits get away with this. If I did, they would rob our other chapels too. So I called on the district magistrate there. I told him that I planned to go talk to the bandit chief myself and tell him to return the mission's property.

" 'I can't let you go alone,' he said, 'because I am responsible for your safety while you are in my jurisdiction. But I will send along with you my most honored corporal with nine soldiers under his command. You tell him what to do, and he will see that his men do it.'

"I didn't really want the ten soldiers, but he insisted.

"The next morning we set off for the little village where the bandit chief lived. Some of the villagers pointed out which house he lived in. Then the corporal stepped up to the door and knocked. No reply. Then he yelled through a crack in the door to the people inside to tell them that the white missionary wished to talk to them and for them to open the door and let him in. Still no reply.

"The second time he gave them a warning, 'Open the door peaceably, or else we will open it.' Again, no answer.

"The soldiers tried to beat down the door with a big log, but they might as well have used a toothpick. The door didn't break." Father paused a moment to think about what had happened.

"That corporal was the bravest Chinese soldier I have ever seen," he said. "His men wanted to give up. They were afraid of what the bandits might do to them later, in revenge. But the corporal ordered his men to get a ladder. Then he climbed up on the roof and took off some tiles. When he had made a large opening, he stationed another soldier on the roof with his rifle pointing down inside. The corporal commanded the soldier to fire if anything went wrong, and then he lowered himself into the bandit's den. Very soon he had the door open.

"When the other soldiers and I entered, we found that the front door had ten six-inch-square concrete posts set in concrete sockets behind the four-inch-thick wooden door. No wonder the soldiers hadn't been able to budge it. It would have taken a cannon to blow it open!

"We found, however, that the people in the house had moved farther back into the building and had barred the doors leading to the area where they had gone."

Father chuckled. "Amidst all this mess, guess who walked in! The bandit chief! The man whose house we were ripping apart!

"And he welcomed us and served us tea just like he was lord of the manor! When we finished, the chief said, 'I am curious, why do such honorable guests call on me today? Is there some way I can serve you?'

"I sent up a quick prayer for guidance. Then I told him that some of his men were making trouble for the mission workers. We all wish to live peaceably together, but the mission needed those things that were taken. And I asked that the stolen property be returned.

" 'My men are very ignorant,' the chief said. 'I shall punish them for doing this. But it will take several days to locate much of the stuff. And some we may have sold and cannot return.'

"I told him to give back what he could, but he would need to pay money for the rest. I asked for the cash to be delivered to my home in Wai Chow in one week.

" 'Give us two weeks,' the chief said, 'as we must go down to the city anyway at that time.'

"I agreed. Now we will see if he delivers."

Florence let out the breath she had been holding during the story. "God is very good, isn't He, Papa? And very strong," she said.

"That He is, child. That He is."

On the appointed day, a messenger from the bandit chief arrived at the gate with the money owed to the mission! God commands respect—even from bandits.

★ ★ ★ ★ ★

Refugees from the countryside poured into Wai Chow, seeking protection from General Chiang's approaching army. They came carrying their belongings on their backs. Some of the elderly had to be carried also, along with the babies and small children who were tired and hungry and screaming in fear. Some of the people had blood running down their bodies from stray bullets. Some had been left to die along the way.

About a hundred Adventist church members came to the compound and begged for refuge. Soon the Nagels' basement was so full of people there was room enough only for each to spread out a mat and sit on the floor. It wasn't safe to be on the upper floors of the house.

Pastor Nagel urged the refugees to go into Wai Chow, telling them they could find more adequate shelter at the girls' school.

Some did go, but others came to take their places. They seemed to find comfort in huddling together.

At different times during the past few years, due to the fighting, Florence and Sonny had spent so many months trying to carry on with their correspondence-school programs while they sat in the basement that they were not looking forward to doing so again—especially surrounded by refugees! Many of Florence's correspondence lessons had been written using a box for a desk and a kerosene lamp for light. Now small children played around her and Sonny. It was definitely not conducive to good studying.

The previous siege had lasted for more than a month. Father had ordered the caretaker to bring the water buffalos and stake them behind the house at the foot of the hill. When there was a lull in the battle, the caretaker would sneak out and milk them. Father had also managed to purchase several large sacks of rice, wheat, dried beans, and peanuts. But before the month was over, all they had left was graham flour. They got down to one meal a day—graham mush. Day after day—graham mush.

Now they were facing another siege, but this time a hundred people sat in their basement, sharing their supplies!

One morning the caretaker said, "One of the buffalos was killed in the fighting last night."

That meant less milk.

Usually the shooting happened only during the daylight hours. At night, mattresses that had been brought down from the second-floor bedrooms to the first floor provided some comfort for a few refugees. The Nagels huddled together and tried to sleep on a rug.

One night, everyone was awakened by blood-curdling screams. The soldiers on top of the city wall opened fire. The next morning the refugees learned that the attacking army had attempted to catch General Yong's troops by surprise. They had tried to scale the city wall with ladders. The battle raged for several hours, and a large number of soldiers were killed.

The next day, Red Cross workers tried to go out between skirmishes and bury the dead, but many of the fallen soldiers lay too far from the shelter of the city wall to be taken care of. The stench became overpowering when the wind blew from that direction.

Finally Pastor Nagel negotiated with officers of the attacking army to permit him and his men to drag the bodies down to the river. Permission was granted. During a short lull in the fighting on both sides, the bodies were disposed of.

Florence hated it when the cannons on the city walls were fired. They shook the house and rattled the windows. Several iron cannon balls came right through the tile roof of the house. Some hit the sides of the building. One bullet even penetrated the iron bedpost of Florence's bed! Another shattered the long mirror in her mother's closet. Every room in the house had bullet holes in the ceiling.

Then suddenly—silence. For several days quiet reigned, even though General Chiang's army was visible not far from the compound. Some of his soldiers were also hiding on the temple grounds outside the city walls.

The Nagels hoped that this silence meant that negotiations were taking place. In fact, Father was approached by General Yong's army. They wanted him to carry a message the next morning to General Chiang Kai-shek.

That day, Florence was studying her correspondence lessons as usual, but she saw no sense in studying down in the basement when it was so calm outside.

"Please, Mother," she begged, "please let me go up to my room and study at my desk. If there is any shooting I'll crawl downstairs quickly. I'll be OK."

Her mother granted permission. How good it was to breathe fresh air again! At her desk, Florence planned to get some serious studying done. Every little while she gazed out the window. But she saw nothing unusual taking place.

Suddenly a man's voice called her. "Get out of this place!" the voice said.

Startled, she looked around to see who was speaking. It wasn't Papa's voice. She knew that for sure. Again the voice spoke, this time with an urgency she couldn't ignore. "Get out of here quickly," the voice commanded.

Florence jumped up and fled. She had barely gotten outside the door to her room when a shot rang out. She heard the singing noise as the bullet sped through the air. She dropped to her knees and crawled down to the basement. Later she found the bullet embedded in her desktop—right in front of where she had been sitting! Psalm 34:7 became an important part of her life from then on: "The angel of the LORD encampeth round about them that fear him, and delivereth them." Florence was convinced that God sent His angel to keep her alive because He had big plans for her future.

A few days later, General Yong's army was able to drive away their attackers, and the refugees were able to safely return to their homes. The Nagels tried to put their household back to normal. Daily lessons were scheduled and rigidly followed; the children must not get behind in their schoolwork. But with invading armies coming to attack so often, the mail service was anything but dependable. Sometimes Florence didn't get her corrected lessons back for six months. Examinations got lost in the mail, and she would have to wait until another set was sent from Washington, D.C. The Andersons were in America on furlough, so the Nagel family was all alone for months at a time. Because a parent wasn't allowed to give the exams, there was no one to give her the tests as the school requested.

One year, Florence took the exams for both the seventh and the eighth grades at the same time. It was a discouraging way to go to school. The correspondence teachers wrote encouraging letters, but it was difficult for her.

Professor M. E. Olsen, principal of the Fireside Correspondence School, often wrote Florence, inspiring her to keep pushing forward. And year after year, the correspondence lessons continued. Florence was grateful for the opportunity to study, but she looked forward to the day when she could go to America and attend a real school.

Three months later, a messenger brought more startling news. "This time General Chiang Kai-shek has the Nationalist Army really equipped," he said. "They have Russian gunners manning the cannons, which they are setting up on the top of a high mountain on the north side of town."

Because the wall around Wai Chow was more than thirty feet high and fifty feet thick at the base, and because a river surrounded the city on three sides, it seemed impregnable. But the messenger was right. This battle was different from all those in the past. It is probably best described in a letter Florence wrote to Professor Olsen of the Fireside Correspondence School during the siege that began just three days before her fifteenth birthday.

October 13, 1925

Dear Professor Olsen:

It is nine o'clock at night. And it's my friend Jean's and my turn to watch the house until midnight. (Jean is actually the dean of girls from Mother's school.) Then it's Mother's turn until three.

We are in the midst of a battle. We are afraid the Nationalist Army will come into this stretch of land where our place is. They are already on three sides of the city. We are between two rivers, so this is always the last place they enter because they cannot get across the wide rivers if an enemy comes in behind them.

Friday morning we were told that the army would be here at four o'clock. We immediately held a prayer meeting, asking that they be delayed until Papa's return. Our prayer was answered that day.

A teacher came from the school and called Mother to go into the city to help them. His wife was about to have a baby. Jean and I went with Mother and closed up the school right away and sent all the boarding students home—all that could go, anyway. Before Jean and I left, we packed up everything we could to get ready for the battle. Then she and I came back to the compound.

Mother was in the city nearly all day. It seemed like that baby was never coming! The gates were locked, and we were afraid the soldiers would not let her come down over the wall.

While she was in the city, one of the generals came out and advised us to move inside the city. I did not know what to say, but finally I told him that we would stay for a while yet.

That night we had all the boarding students that were left stay up at our house for fear of trouble during the night.

Sabbath morning came, and no army yet. When it was time for Sabbath School, I went into the city to get some of the former students who still attended Sabbath School. The gates were all locked except one. There was not much trouble during the day—until four o'clock, when they again said that the army was coming. But it did not come—in answer to more of our prayers, I'm sure.

On Sunday they said the army would be here at one o'clock, but it didn't come. I wished it would never come— or hurry up and come!

Monday morning the army had not yet arrived. Two of our pastors came down from a chapel only six miles away, and they said that the army had arrived there at ten o'clock the night before. That frightened us because we knew this was news—not rumor.

Tuesday morning the real battle began. The Nationalist Army at last arrived. The first guns went off while I was working in the garden. We were very glad that it was on the west side of the city, but everybody was afraid. We could see the soldiers on the hills.

Much to our sorrow, about an hour later we found out for sure that the army had brought cannons. This is the first time in several years that the army has brought cannons.

At eleven o'clock the army was on the north side of the house, across the river. The firing was so heavy that we had to stay in the basement. During this time the authorities forbade anyone to go in or out of the city.

At noon the fighting was very severe, and it lasted until the sun went down. Neither side gained anything.

Before this battle began, a wedding procession came out of Wai Chow through Convenient Gate, the gate nearest us. When the people went out to get the bride, there was no battle. Now they could not get back into the city, so the coolies set the bride chair by our front gate and went to see what they could do about it. I felt sorry for the poor girl. None of her family or friends stayed with her, and she could not get out of the special sedan chair brides are carried in.

The people finally decided to get a big ladder and take her up over the wall. They took off her traditional red wedding dress, and while she was going over the wall, bullets flew all around her.

The chair coolies did not have any rope, and the soldiers would not let them take the chair into the city through a gate, so she had to walk to her new home. Because she was not very pretty, everyone laughed at her.

About three o'clock we had nearly decided that we would leave the compound and go into the city. The reason we were so anxious was that Monday evening General Yong called to us from the wall and said we were not to let the army on our compound. He said they were very bad soldiers and if they came in, he would shoot the cannons right on us. But how could we keep an army off if they should decide to come in?

In addition to all the rest, a plane flew over this afternoon and dropped a few bombs on Wai Chow—at least they were aiming for Wai Chow, I'm sure. But only one bomb landed inside the city walls. We are praying hard for protection here.

Bullets were flying everywhere this evening while we talked to General Yong about going into the city. Now he changed his mind and begged us to stay on the compound and protect it for them, so that General Chiang's army would not come into the compound and use the houses for forts. We agreed to stay, and he promised not to turn the big guns on us after all. We felt a little safer.

The sun has gone down now, and Papa has not come home yet. We are getting very worried, for he promised to be back about three o'clock today.

All the workers on the compound have come to stay at our house with Sonny and Jean and me. We have set a time for everyone to stand guard during the night. Jean and I are taking the nine-to-midnight watch. (Jean is my sister—not a real one, but she seems just like one of the family.)

Later—

Well, I was aroused from writing my letter last night by a noise at our front door. It frightened me, but I went to the window to see what it was. I thought it was one of the generals coming to ask some questions or something like that.

There were two people sleeping upstairs, and they also heard the noise and came down to open the door. Papa had come! You cannot imagine how happy I was.

We did not know it, but some of General Chiang's army had come onto a stretch of land by our compound. They had been so quiet and had done no shooting, so we didn't know they were here. Papa had to go through their lines. He didn't dare to bring the horses with them, so he left them with General Chiang's army. Papa told us that the part of General Chiang's army closest to us was made up of young farm boys who were beginning students at the Canton Military Training School—not hardened soldiers. So we all relaxed and went to bed. But I think this was the worst day I have ever lived through. Jean said she had never heard so many cannons in her life.

This morning when we woke up, the army by the side of our compound had moved back, we don't know why. They are very quiet on all the other sides, too.

A little while ago, some people came from the city, carrying out the dead who were killed by the bomb yesterday. The people in the city are scared to death of the airplanes. When they drop bombs, it is always the people who suffer. Very seldom do bombs kill soldiers.

Papa arranged with the army to let our horses, hostler, and coolies leave the temple across from our compound at seven o'clock, and that the city soldiers would be ordered not to fire at anything during that time. We waited anxiously for over an hour, but they didn't come. We feared the army was not going to let them come.

Much to our joy, a little after eight we saw the hostler sneaking along in the bamboo with the stars and stripes floating over his head and the horses and coolies following. The city soldiers did not fire. The baggage was all there, too. And the flour, sugar, potatoes, and other food supplies. We are very thankful for God's love and care.

General Chiang's army concentrated all its forces on the weakest place in the city wall. Cannon ball after cannon ball was hurled at the North Gate. No human being could stand before such firing. The army battered down the city wall low enough so that they could easily scale it with ladders. Then into the city they went, fighting their way. I've been told that North Gate is all shot to pieces. Gunfire continues heavy.

We were eating our dinner when someone came to tell us that soldiers were crossing the river in front of the city. We left dinner and ran out to see. Bullets were flying everywhere. We soon discovered the soldiers were crossing the river to scale the city walls from this side too.

The Wai Chow soldiers from the wall came running into the compound, pleading with us to save their lives. We had the kitchen door open, and several ran into the house and hid. One even dumped the wood out of the box by the stove and crawled under it. They threw their guns under the chairs and dripped blood on our living-room rug. We finally got the door shut. Then we had the job of getting the frightened soldiers out of our house. We took them to the back gate of the compound and told them to run for their lives because there was no army out that way yet.

Such an hour we never want to pass through again—men kneeling before us, pleading for their lives, and we were unable to help. We told them that if they stayed with us they would be shot as soon as the other army entered the city. And we would be in a lot of trouble, too.

The blood ran down their faces, arms, and legs. Oh, it was a terrible sight! One died standing in front of the church. Three of them climbed up into the bell tower, pulled the rope up after them, and stayed up there until

Ruins of the North Gate where more than four hundred soldiers were killed in the fighting.

dark. Many hid in the barn, under logs, in the greenhouse, and in almost every conceivable place.

We're told that there are about four hundred dead people at the North Gate and that the whole city is full of wounded soldiers. One general got away from the city with several hundred soldiers when he saw that his soldiers could not stand up to the fighting. They fled out over the wall nearest to our compound. I hear that hundreds of his soldiers threw their guns into the ponds and dressed up in coolie clothes, so the Nationalist Army would not know they were soldiers. Many fled into private homes and hid their guns. Unfortunately some of the soldiers ran into our girls' school, hiding their guns there also. Later when the Nationalist Army searched the city, they robbed only from the homes—or schools—where they found guns. At our school most of our supplies were stolen.

Later—

Yesterday about six thousand soldiers passed by our place. Today several thousand more left. The fighting is not very far away now.

Many of our students thought they would be safer in the school, so they went back there not knowing that guns were hidden in the desks and cabinets. So when the school was robbed, those students lost all the clothes and food they had brought with them.

Things are still unsettled. We do not know what to expect next. But we are of good courage, knowing that God still rules. And tomorrow is my fifteenth birthday!

With love,
Florence Nagel

Pastor Nagel and General Chiang Kai-shek. The day after Wai Chow fell to the Nationalist Army, Pastor Nagel called on the general to tell him of the many guns that had been left on the mission compound.

P.S. I haven't been able to mail this letter yet, so I wanted to tell you the latest thing that's happened. Yesterday, Papa and a Chinese pastor went to the military headquarters in the city. They were able to speak with General Chiang Kai-shek himself. Papa explained his situation and asked the general to send soldiers to the compound to collect the guns that the army left there. Then Papa had his picture taken with the general! He's going to keep it in his passport. He says it will be a great help in carrying on his work. When officials stop him and find that picture, they surely will allow him to go wherever he needs to.

Florence.

CHAPTER EIGHT

Birthday Parties and Executions

The government of Wai Chow had fallen to General Chiang Kai-shek's troops, and there was unrest in the countryside. General Yong's former soldiers now became robbers, controlling travel on the roads and rivers. No one was safe anywhere.

Pastor Nagel decided to take his family to Hong Kong and leave them there until the situation cleared up. The strain of living in the war zone was taking its toll. They needed a break from the death and destruction that had been surrounding them constantly during the last three years.

Boat travel was impossible, and only one road out of the city was reported to be "safe" to travel. Even on it, the robbers often stopped travelers and extracted a toll for "guaranteed safe passage."

However, Pastor Nagel decided to chance it. He set a date for their departure. When that morning came, the hostler saddled four horses and packed the mules in the predawn hours; the party started out as soon as it was light.

After an entire day in the saddle, Florence barely managed to walk when they arrived at the inn where they would spend the night. She was tired and saddle sore. She looked at Mother and Sonny; they also showed signs of weariness. Only Papa seemed unfazed by the ride. But of course, he often rode a horse when he visited the mission chapels.

Soon the innkeeper set bowls of steaming rice and plates of fresh green peas and scrambled eggs before them. Florence ate heartily but almost fell asleep before she finished.

The exhausted travelers soon climbed the steps to the bedroom above the kitchen. The open latticework of the floor permitted the warmth of the kitchen fires to flow into their room—but it also allowed the smoke to enter! In the room, they found board beds with straw mats and mosquito nets hanging over them. The nets were almost black from absorbing soot over the years. But to Florence, Sonny, Mother, and Father, any place to lie down looked inviting.

Florence had been lying on her bed for only a short time when she felt something crawling all over her body.

"Papa!" she whispered anxiously. "Something's in my bed!"

Father lit a small kerosene lamp, and together they started to clean the bedbugs from her straw mat. At first they made a game of it by counting each bedbug they killed, but after reaching a hundred, they lost count. Just when they thought they had them all, more seemed to pop up out of nowhere. And the whole procedure had to be repeated. They spent most of that night killing bedbugs.

Travelers who did not have rooms slept on mats on the ground floor. Before they settled down, they smoked for a while—both cigarettes and opium. This smoke also floated up through the flooring into the rooms above. So between chasing bedbugs and breathing the foul smoke from below, the Nagels spent a mostly sleepless night. They eagerly awaited dawn, so they could be on their way again, out in the fresh air.

The next morning, their caravan of four horses, two mules, the hostler, and several coolies carrying baggage came to a shallow river about an hour into their journey. A dark gray mule called Stubby (for "stubborn") was in the lead. True to his breed, he balked, refusing to go through the stream. When Stubby was forced to go, he waded reluctantly to the middle of the stream and stopped. He turned and looked back. First, he brayed at the people watching. Then he lay down in the muddy water and rolled from side to side, completely soaking the suitcases and bundles on his back.

When they all reached the opposite bank, Father held up his hand. "We'll stop here," he called out. "Let's unpack the suitcases and dry out the clothes."

As Mother spread out the last dress on the grass, she wiped her forehead. "I thank the good Lord that this isn't the wet season, or else it would take two days to dry."

Several hours later, they packed up the dry clothes and started out again. Later in the morning, the black stallion Father rode caught one of his hoofs in a loose board on a badly repaired bridge. The accident tore the skin on his leg, and it started bleeding. For the next few hours, the caravan moved slowly as Blacky limped the rest of the way with Father walking beside him.

They finally reached the port city of Sa Ng Chun. It was a welcome sight. Usually when Pastor Nagel traveled this way, the hostler stayed in this town with the horses until Father returned from Hong Kong. But this time the hostler would spend the night and return to Wai Chow the next day.

The boat they needed to take had not left yet, but it was already overcrowded with passengers. Baskets of pigs and cages of chickens were piled on the front deck along with the other baggage. Because the Nagels were the last passengers to get on, they had to sit on their own baggage beside the pigs and chickens. Fortunately the trip took only three hours.

The ocean was rough, and the waves crested higher than usual. By the time the boat reached Tai Po Market in the New Territories of Hong Kong, many of the passengers were thoroughly seasick.

At Tai Po Market, the Nagels boarded a train to the city of Kowloon. Then a ferry took them across Victoria Harbor to the city of Hong Kong. After a ride up the steep hill in a tram car, they finally arrived at Uncle Lee's house just as the sun set over the water and the distant hills. It had been a very long two days!

Father established the family in a vacant apartment and began his return trip to Wai Chow the next day. The Andersons were still away on furlough, and he was concerned about what might be happening at home.

In Hong Kong, Florence found that many of the Christian youth worked during their summer holiday selling Christian books to earn scholarships for the next school year. Fifteen-year-old Florence received permission from the Union Office to sell books also. She was assigned a partner, and they started to work.

When they walked into the first shop, Florence spoke to the shopkeeper in Chinese, telling him of her books about the wonderful Savior named Jesus. The shopkeeper stood open-mouthed while she talked.

"Missy speaks Chinese!" he said when she paused for a breath. "How is this?"

Soon she had sold him a book. He was still staring in amazement when she left his shop. This scene was repeated in many shops in the following weeks.

Toward the end of September, the mission headquarters and the missionary families moved into a brand-new modern housing site called Felix Villas on the east side of Victoria Island. Every apartment had a breathtaking view of the islands and the bay. And the missionaries' children thoroughly enjoyed the private swimming beach and its floating pier with a diving board. Florence spent many happy hours there—and one not so happy hour.

One day she was diving off the floating pier with a friend when Mother called them to come in for supper.

"Please, Mother," Florence begged, "can we take just one more dive?" The friend dove first; Florence followed.

Suddenly Florence felt something wrapping around her foot and another something wrapping itself around her right arm. By kicking she was able to release her foot, and with her left hand she managed to free her right arm. But before she reached the shore, her hand was so swollen her fingers resembled bananas. And the pain was so intense she was crying. Mother took one look at her swelling limbs and grabbed Florence by the arm and ran for the doctor's house half a block away. Within minutes of arriving at the doctor's house, Florence began to lose feeling in her arms. Then the paralysis crept down to her legs. The doctor said she'd been stung or bitten by something in the water, and the poison was acting as an anesthetic. He hoped it was only temporary. Lots of prayers were said for her that evening.

The next morning, fishermen dredged the area and caught an enormous octopus. Fortunately, Florence recovered within a few days.

★ ★ ★ ★ ★

Sweet sixteen! Florence counted the days until her birthday. In China, a girl is considered an adult at sixteen, ready for marriage. Florence wasn't interested in marriage, but being sixteen was special. Even Uncle Victor and Aunt Letha had come down from Canton for her birthday—and for a few days of vacation.

In 1926, October 16 came on Sabbath. Florence awoke with a feeling of anticipation. This was *her* day!

In Hong Kong, the English-speaking Adventists met for Sabbath services in a home in the afternoon—both missionaries and English-speaking Chinese. After the service, Pastor Paul Williams, the Union treasurer, suggested they all take a walk in the Happy Valley Cemetery. It was one of the most beautiful spots on the island with its many flowering shrubs. Big shade trees blossomed in pink and white. A fountain and a lily pond marked the entrance to the grounds. Usually Florence enjoyed walking on the trails and reading the inscriptions on the sculptured tombstones. But not today.

Of all the places to spend my sixteenth birthday! she grumbled to herself. *Why must I go to a cemetery? Doesn't anyone remember it's my birthday?*

Once in Happy Valley, Florence drifted away from the group. She wanted to be alone. First she went to the tomb of Abram La Rue. Her mind pictured the days when he first came to Hong Kong. On resurrection morning when the Lord raises him from the dead, she wanted to meet Mr. La Rue and ask him a few questions. She was curious to know what gave him the burning desire to leave America and come alone halfway around the world. For fifteen years he worked on the docks to support himself while he shared his faith with the Chinese people. He had been buried on this lonely hillside just six years before Florence was born.

Florence wandered to other tombs with names she recognized. Doctors, ministers, teachers—she'd heard stories about them all.

They were the real pioneers of the mission work. They came to China because they loved the Lord and wanted to share His goodness with others. There were the graves also of women who came to help their husbands, then died in childbirth because proper medical help wasn't available. Florence stood looking out over the bay and thought of others. There was Pastor Edwin Wilbur who died in 1914. She had no personal memory of him, but she had heard the story many times of how he came to Wai Chow to bring her and her mother to safety in Canton. About the United States submarine that had been sent to look for them. Pastor Wilbur wasn't buried here, but at the resurrection, she'd finally meet him. How surprised he'd be to meet the infant he'd rescued from Wai Chow! She thought about Amanda Anderson, Helen and Hazel's mother, buried in faraway Shanghai.

As Florence thought back over the sixteen years of her own life, she began to capture the spirit of these pioneers. There in that cemetery on the hill she rededicated her life to the task of hastening Christ's return. She would finish her education and come back to China as soon as possible. No, not here in Hong Kong. Hong Kong wasn't the real China that she loved. She wanted to go to the interior, back to her old home by the walled city of Wai Chow, back to the people she could speak with in their own language. She could help them; she knew she could.

Well, she thought, *maybe this is a wonderful way to celebrate my sixteenth birthday after all.*

When they all went back to their homes, her mind kept turning over and over the vow

Florence the day following her sixteenth birthday, when she wrote the poem, "I'm Going Back to China." That poem would prove to be a guiding motif in her life.

she had just made to her heavenly Father. As soon as possible she slipped away to her room and began to write what was on her heart. After several starts, she chewed on her eraser a moment and then began to write again:

I'M GOING BACK
TO CHINA

I'm going back to China
No more from duty wander.
My heart turns back to China;
I can stay here no longer.
I miss the old walled city,
My home and childhood country.
My heart's gone back to China,
And I must go!

I'm traveling back to China;
My step is fast—not feeble.
I pray the Lord to help me
And keep me from all evil.
I know my Guide will lead me
To where bright crowns await me.
My heart's gone back to China,
And I must go!

I'm going back to China.
I'm going back to China.
I'm going where the cotton trees grow.
For I hear the heathen calling,
My childhood friends a-calling.
My heart's gone back to China,
And I must go!

When she finished, Florence reread the words. Truly, they expressed her heart. She would keep that piece of paper and read it whenever her life seemed to be heading in another direction.

After sundown worship with the other missionaries, Pastor Williams said, "I have an announcement to make. Today is Florence Nagel's sixteenth birthday, and you're all invited to go with us down to the Blue Bird Restaurant for a special dessert."

Florence gasped. She was sure everyone had forgotten about her birthday. How wrong she was! At the Blue Bird Restaurant, Florence had her first taste of a delicacy that had just been introduced into Hong Kong—Eskimo Pies. As she licked the chocolate coating and the vanilla ice cream ran down the stick onto her hand, she smiled to herself. They hadn't forgotten her birthday after all.

The next morning her mother asked for her help. "Please help me set up these folding tables in the living room, will you?"

"Sure, Mother," Florence responded. "But why? Are we having company?"

Mother smiled. "We certainly are," she said. "Twenty guests are coming for dinner." She paused, then went over and put her arms around Florence. "My dear child, did you really think we had forgotten your birthday? We're going to have a party!"

And it was a wonderful party! Besides the cards and gifts the guests brought, there were letters and packages sent by family and old friends.

No, her birthday definitely hadn't been forgotten. It turned out to be a truly memorable sixteenth birthday.

★ ★ ★ ★ ★

The Andersons returned from furlough in November, leaving Pastor Nagel free to rejoin his family in Hong Kong. It was exciting to have him with them, but Florence noticed something strange in his expression. And he changed the subject whenever she asked, "When can we go back home, Papa?"

Finally he sat the family down and began talking to them. He explained how the family had been in only one mission field for so many years and that they needed a change. He had already asked the China Division Office in Shanghai for a transfer. Their personal belongings were already packed up and on their way to Hong Kong. Their furniture and kitchen things—even Florence's beloved piano—had been sold.

Florence was devastated. "Oh, no, Papa!" she cried. "How could you? Where will we go?"

Her father cleared his throat. "I have been invited to be the pastor of the church in Kuala Lumpur in Malaysia," he said. "I've also been asked to be the director of the mission work in the Swatow area. So we have two choices."

"Please don't make us leave China," Florence pleaded. "Please, please take the one in Swatow. I don't want to leave China, Papa—not until I go to college."

Father accepted the position in Swatow. As soon as their belongings arrived from Wai Chow, he booked passage for the family on an ocean liner for the overnight trip to Swatow.

The city of Swatow was a far cry from Wai Chow. Some might say it was a step up for the Nagels. To begin with, Swatow was a coastal city, between Hong Kong and Amoy. The city had quite modern stores, electricity in the homes, and wide roads with automobiles and trucks on them—in addition to bicycles, horses, and pedestrians.

This is all very nice, Florence thought, *but it's not Wai Chow.*

Swatow was built on flat delta land. Gone were the rolling hills that Florence loved. Gone were the friends she'd grown up with. Gone was the home she'd loved. And gone was the language she understood. In Swatow, people spoke a different kind of Chinese—a dialect she would have to learn.

Florence sighed.

Sonny took one look at the compound and whispered to her, "I want to go home."

They soon discovered they faced more than just homesickness. The mission compound at Swatow was located in a busy area. It was a mile out of town, but a canal from the ocean ran in front of the property. It was an active waterway, always full of sampans and tenders carrying freight from the ships in the harbor to the railroad station beyond the mission compound. Just outside the east wall of the compound a large kiln burned sea shells twenty-four hours a day to make lime. The smoke frequently caused the Nagels' eyes to sting and become bloodshot. And the smoke-filled air was difficult to breathe. On the opposite side of the compound, a factory made a sauce from rotten fish. The noise from these two factories made it difficult to concentrate on anything else.

In addition to all of this, semiweekly executions took place nearby, announced by bugle blasts. And though Florence and Sonny crawled under the covers and put their fingers in their ears, they couldn't shut out the noise of the rifles when the executions took place. Then the relatives of the condemned prisoners would bring coffins out to the vacant lot behind the compound and go through the wailing and the rituals for the dead for several hours. Florence's heart hurt for the mourners, and she remembered her promise to God on her sixteenth birthday. Someday she would be a grown-up missionary and tell these people that Jesus was coming again soon.

No, Swatow wasn't Wai Chow. When her parents had moved to Wai Chow, their house was brand new. Here in Swatow, the two houses on the compound had problems. A few years earlier, a tidal wave had drenched them, and the salty ocean water had soaked into the limestone walls. And because Swatow was a coastal city with high humidity, the walls never completely dried out. Now, mold continually fell off the walls, leaving a white film of dust by the mop boards. The mold had a peculiar, unpleasant odor. An even stronger odor came from in front of their house where many coolies used the shore daily for their toilet.

But the Nagels were missionaries, and they needed to act like it. Mother soon had everything unpacked. She succeeded in turning this smelly pile of limestone into an inviting home for her family and their new friends. She also had Florence and Sonny back on their study schedule—with one addition: a language teacher. Several hours every morning a man named Wong Tin Chin came to teach them the Swatowese language.

Swatow did have one advantage. When Father visited the small chapels and schools around his territory, he was away for only short periods. And he could travel by boat or train—not by horseback or on foot.

Mother soon became involved in the local school. She loved working with the teachers and students. Florence also taught some of the subjects. In this way the Nagels became acquainted with the people and soon formed many new friendships.

They had been in Swatow about six months when rumors reached them that General Chiang Kai-shek's army was nearing Swatow. Some said he would attack by boat; others reported he was coming by train. Father needed to visit some of the churches farther up the coast, so he asked the American consulate if it would be permissible for him to leave town at this time.

The consul replied, "You know the ways of the Chinese military better than I do. But my idea is that it will be a while before they arrive. Don't be gone too long, and let me know when you return."

That Friday morning Florence and a friend went down to the wharf to tell her father goodbye. The girls did some shopping in the noisy, bustling downtown before they returned home to get ready for Sabbath.

When the family awoke in the morning, a strange stillness surrounded them. There was no activity at either factory, no coolies on the beach, no movement, no sound. What had happened? Where was everybody?

CHAPTER NINE

This Strange New World

That morning, Florence was the Sabbath School superintendent, so she left a little early to have everything prepared at church.
Pastor and Mrs. Newcombe, the missionaries in the other house on
the compound, joined Florence as she left. As they walked, they
were the only people on the road. It was eerie.

Suddenly, they saw one of the church members running toward
them, shouting and waving his arms in the air.

"Hurry! Hurry! Come quickly!" he said. "Our church is on
fire! And the soldiers won't let anyone put it out!"

During the night, General Chiang Kai-shek and the Nationalist
Army had sneaked into town and surprised everyone. No battle
was fought. In the morning the people found that General Chiang
had posted sentries at all government buildings, including a large
storage depot holding weapons and government records—right next
door to the Seventh-day Adventist Church.

As Florence and the Newcombes ran toward the church, they
saw smoke rising above the structures. Then they saw the flames.
But it wasn't the church that was burning—not yet anyway. To
keep the enemy from having access to the depot, the fleeing
Swatow soldiers had set fire to the storage warehouse. Flames
enveloped the building, and the wind was blowing them toward
the roof of the church. Any minute it would catch on fire too.

The Nationalist Army refused to allow anyone to call the fire department.

Pastor Newcombe gathered the small group of believers right in the street in front of the church, and they prayed earnestly that God would perform a miracle before all these unbelievers. With strong faith, they chorused "Amen" and looked toward the fire. God was working a miracle right that minute! The wind had changed direction! Now it was blowing the flames away from the church. Florence felt a thrill run down her spine. But the fire was still right next door.

Just then a fire engine pushed its way through the crowd of onlookers, fire bell clanging. One of the Adventist members, Dr. Ang, was riding on the running board. In spite of the Nationalist soldiers' commands, he had slipped away to the headquarters of the new government and discovered that the officer in charge was an old schoolmate of his. When the officer heard what was happening, he gave orders to send the fire department to protect the church from burning. Once on the scene, the firemen quickly hooked up the hoses and pointed them toward the church walls, roof, and the window openings. The danger to the church was soon past.

Many of the onlookers brought buckets and rags to help mop up the water-soaked sanctuary. Pastor Newcombe invited everyone to join them for the Sabbath services. And Sabbath School began with a packed church.

Florence didn't follow the program she had planned for that morning. Instead, she turned the meeting into a praise service, and many people thanked God for His marvelous protection.

★ ★ ★ ★ ★

The summer before Florence turned eighteen, she completed all the requirements for the twelfth grade. The president of the Fireside Correspondence School, China Division, made arrangements for her to go to Shanghai and take part in the graduation exercises with the first class of students to graduate from the newly formed Far Eastern Academy. This was exciting! Florence looked forward to joining other students and taking part in a real graduation. It was more than she'd dreamed of. And after that—America! Florence eagerly awaited the time when she would go to America to college. After all, she had made a promise to the Lord. She needed an education before she could return to China to share her love for God with the people in Wai Chow. And it needed to be Pacific Union College.

Then her mother became ill—dangerously ill. Day by day her condition deteriorated.

"Little Lotus Blossom," her father said one day, "I need your help. Mother is getting worse, and the doctor says he's done all he can. She must be taken to the Shanghai Sanitarium. I can't leave right now, so I need you to go with her. Stay right by her side and help take care of her." He took a deep breath and repeated it for emphasis. "Don't leave her side."

Florence felt sick at heart. She loved her mother, but she had dreamed of graduating with the students at Far Eastern Academy. Now that wouldn't happen. Oh, well, there was still college at the end of the summer.

"Yes, Papa," she said, trying to muster up a smile. "I'll take good care of Mother."

Even in Shanghai, however, her mother's condition worsened. Nothing helped her. And Florence was exhausted. Finally one of the nurses sent her to bed.

"You'll be a patient next if you don't get some rest," she said. "I'll stay with your mother tonight."

Later that night, Dr. Woods came to Florence's room and woke her up.

"Your mother needs you," he said. "Will you go down to her bedside and tell her you will not go to America this summer as you planned? She is sick with worry about your leaving. It is troubling her so much we can't promise she will pull through the night." How could this be? She had promised God to get herself ready to serve Him! And now she couldn't? Florence was tired of studying alone, tired of taking all her courses by correspondence. But she couldn't be the cause of her mother's death, could she? And Mother would need her care if she pulled through the night. It would be a long road to recovery.

Florence finally stood up and threw her shoulders back and marched down the stairs to her mother's room. She knelt by her mother's bed and gently took her hand.

"I'm here, Mother," she said softly. "And I'll stay right here beside you until you are well. I won't go to PUC this year . . ." She swallowed the lump in her throat. "I'll help you get better. You will get better, won't you?"

Slowly her mother's condition improved. And in the few weeks before they returned to Swatow, Florence sadly went down to the wharf to say goodbye when the students sailed to America to attend college. Florence felt a dark cloud of discouragement hanging over her. Why couldn't she go too? She needed to go, didn't she?

When Pastor Nagel took his wife and daughter back to Swatow, Florence enrolled in a nursing course by correspondence from the Chicago School of Nursing. Whether or not she became a nurse, her time wouldn't be completely wasted because PUC had agreed to accept the classes she was enrolled in. So she would enter PUC as a sophomore.

Florence tried to be interested in nursing, but she just couldn't put her heart into it. She didn't want to become a nurse—especially by correspondence. She wanted to go to college in America with her friends. She wanted to prepare to be a . . . uh . . . doctor? . . . Bible worker? Well, what she really wanted was to return to China with a husband by her side. A missionary wife! That's what she'd prepare to be. Then she could really be of service to the people of China.

Miss Ida Thompson, a missionary teacher, had talked with her several times. "You must never come back single, my dear," Miss Thompson told her. "It is such a lonely life in a foreign land when you're single."

So why did God seem to want her here in Swatow this extra year?

★ ★ ★ ★ ★

In Swatow, Mary Nagel rapidly recovered, and she soon was going about her customary duties: taking care of her house and her family, and supervising the school for Chinese children. Early one morning a messenger raced to the compound and urged her to go to the school immediately. When she arrived, Mrs. Nagel found one of the young teachers on the floor, unconscious. Within hours she died.

Her husband, Tan Kia O, was away on a business trip. No one knew where to reach him, so he didn't learn of his wife's death until he returned home. He was crushed by the devastating news. For some time he could not be comforted.

The Nagel family told Mr. Tan they would care for his three children until other arrangements could be made. He had a six-year-old son, and two little girls, one five, the other only three.

This turned out to be a blessing for Florence. Having the children in her home gave her something besides lessons and disappointment to think about. She gave the three-year-old the English name of Edith and loved to play with her and care for her. When the older children were at school, little Edith played with her toys on the floor nearby while Florence studied. Edith became Florence's shadow. When the older children were at home, Florence took them for walks, taught them songs, and helped them with their studies. She even enjoyed sewing for them. The children stayed with the Nagel family for a year.

Florence herself grew up a lot that year. Not in stature, however. No matter how tall she stood she would never measure more than five feet, one inch tall. This wasn't a disadvantage in southern China, however, because she fit right in with the people around her. But she grew in maturity, in patience, and in an understanding of God and her fellow men.

Instead of sending his children to America for school, Pastor Nagel decided to take the whole family to America so that Florence and Sonny could live at home and attend school. They planned also to take Joseph Hwang with them. Joseph was a young man who worked at the mission. For several years he had been saving money and dreaming of one day going to college in America. Pastor Nagel had made all the arrangements for Joseph's visa to the United States and his entrance to college.

So once again, Florence began planning and dreaming of attending college—with classmates and professors. Often Florence, Sonny, and Joseph talked about going to America to school. Sonny would finish high school there and then join Florence and Joseph in college. When the PUC bulletin came, they spent hours together happily planning their courses.

Four months before the Nagels planned to sail for America, word came that Mr. Tan had been kidnapped and was being held for ransom. Weeks passed, and no satisfactory terms were reached. The mission could not pay the ransom money. If they did, all the workers could be kidnapped and held for ransom. None would be safe. Mr. Tan's parents or brothers, however, did not have the large sum of money demanded for his release.

Joseph Hwang, with the children of his brother-in-law, Tan Kia O, who was kidnapped and held for ransom.

Joseph Hwang was Mr. Tan's brother-in-law. And Joseph had the money, but it was earmarked for his own education. What should he do? Should he sacrifice his future education and use the money to free his brother-in-law? Two months passed, and Mr. Tan was still a prisoner. Finally Joseph paid the ransom and watched the joyous reunion his brother-in-law had with his children. Mr. Tan looked terrible. He was thin and sickly looking, but everyone thanked God for preserving him.

Joseph never got to study in America, but he did become a pastor. And eventually he became a missionary to the Philippines, where he pastored the Chinese church in Manila. He also served as the assistant chaplain of the Manila Sanitarium and Hospital.

As the date drew near for the Nagels to sail for America, Florence approached her father. "Please, Papa," she begged, "may I go back to Wai Chow and see all my friends again? I don't know when I'll have another chance to see them."

Her father stroked his chin. "Yes, I think that can be arranged. You can go right after the Union meetings in Canton are finished."

She checked off the days on her calendar, looking forward with keen anticipation. In the meantime, she helped her mother pack all their belongings. This time, it was not just a furlough they were taking. The Nagel family was moving to America—leaving China. For Florence, the two years of anxious waiting were almost over. Her courage and faith grew stronger. She prayed earnestly that she would not be disappointed this time.

At the Union meetings, everyone knew that the Nagels were leaving. Many of her friends asked Florence, "You will return, won't you, Lotus Blossom?"

"Oh, yes," she replied. "I plan to be gone only three years."

To a few, she confided more of her dream. "I've asked God to arrange a good companion for me," she told them. "Then we will come back together and join you all here in China."

Florence had kept Miss Thompson's words in her heart and prayed that God would guide in every step of her future plans. She must prepare herself to be the best missionary's wife she could be. And she kept in her mind the words she wrote on her sixteenth birthday: "I'm going back to China . . . and I must go!"

When the meetings were over, quite a few workers wanted to go to Wai Chow with Florence. They rode the ferry upriver to Sa Ng Chung. Instead of horses to meet them, a road had been built and old Ford trucks were there to take passengers on to Wai Chow. The road hadn't been completed yet, so when they reached an unfinished bridge, the passengers rode a ferry across the river, then they all boarded a battered bus waiting on the other side. With all the people and baggage, the bus was heavily loaded. Some even sat on top, and others stood on the running boards, hanging on to anything they could grab. When they came to a steep hill, the passengers had to walk. But every hill, every river, brought them closer to Wai Chow.

Florence's heart beat faster as she neared her old home for the first time in three years. When they rounded the last curve and the whole city came into view, Florence gasped! She could see their old compound and the river that divided the city—but where were the city walls? Those thirty-foot high walls? She soon found that the walls had been taken down to make room for wide paved roads around the two halves of the city—roads with cars and buses on them. There were bridges spanning the river! And even a few tall modern buildings.

Florence thought of the time Uncle Victor had ridden his motorcycle up from Canton. He had taken her for a ride through the city—her first ride on a motorized vehicle. The chickens scattered and squawked, the dogs barked, the pigs squealed, and the children had run for their lives. The next day a courier came from the magistrate's office. He requested they never ride the motorcycle in town again. It would scare all the spirits, and they might bring great revenge. Florence smiled now as she remembered it all. *I wonder what the spirits think of all these changes?* she thought.

Even on the compound, changes had taken place. A third mission house had been built, and all three homes now had electricity and telephone service.

Florence visited old friends and saw old familiar places. In some cases, she searched for a familiar place only to find it had been torn down to make way for "progress." She enjoyed her time in Wai Chow. Too soon the day came to say goodbye to everyone in Wai Chow. Florence tempered the sadness with the solemn promise to return as soon as she finished her schooling.

When Florence returned to Canton, there were more Goodbyes to say. But it wasn't a sad parting. She planned to be back in a very few years. And in the meantime, she was bound for PUC. She could hardly wait to get there. Sonny would be starting his tenth grade in the academy, and Florence her second year in college. Both were excited and a little nervous. What would school be like?

The Nagel family shortly before leaving China for the United States. Florence planned on returning to China in a few years after completing her college work in America. She little knew what the years ahead would hold!

★ ★ ★ ★ ★

On the *SS Korea Maru* the Nagels weren't the only Adventist missionaries bound for America. Uncle Victor (Mother's brother), Aunt Letha, and their children were with them. Also on the ship were Ellen G. White's twin grandsons, Herbert and Henry White, and their families.

Throughout the voyage, the ship's officers arranged activities and sports for the passengers to enjoy. Florence played deck golf so well that the captain often asked her to be his partner. The time sped by, and suddenly it was time for the sports tournament that signaled the end of the trip. Usually it was held on the last Saturday of the voyage, but in deference to all the Adventists on board, the tournament was scheduled for the last Monday. Florence and Uncle Victor won in shuffleboard, and Florence won the championship in deck golf.

At the Captain's Dinner on the last night of the trip, the prizes for the tournament were given out, and Florence received her prize—a camera! What a wonderful gift for a college-bound girl! Then the captain gave a little speech, saying he had a few passengers to whom he wished to give special gifts.

He cleared his throat. "I have been especially challenged by the aptitude and quickness of a certain young lady on this voyage. She is a good partner in any sport, and a wicked foe if she's not on my side." The listeners chuckled. Then he picked up a bag and pulled out a beautiful Japanese kimono. "Florence Nagel," he said, "please come up here."

The audience broke into applause as the captain draped the kimono over the shoulders of the tongue-tied girl. Many of them knew firsthand her skill and sportsmanship. The next morning Florence was out on deck early. She wanted to watch the ship sail through the Golden Gate and into San Francisco Bay. Grandma Nagel waited on the dock with hugs and kisses for everybody.

The ship would lay over in San Francisco for two days and then the Nagels would reboard and sail on to Los Angeles. But two days were enough for Mother and Aunt Letha to go by bus to Angwin, the little town built around Pacific Union College. They each needed to rent a house for their families for the coming school year.

Father and Uncle Victor took Grandma Nagel and the children for some sightseeing around the city. On Sabbath they ran into old friends at the Capp Street Seventh-day Adventist Church. Late Saturday night the women returned from Angwin, their mission accomplished. On Sunday morning they said Goodbye to Grandma and boarded the ship again. The ship sailed south, following the coastline.

In Los Angeles, all the aunts and uncles and cousins stood with Grandfather and Grandmother Hansen, waiting at the pier as the ship pulled in. What a family reunion!

Toward the end of their month-long visit with the family, Father bought a little Model A Ford. Every morning he and Florence took driving lessons. Florence was appalled by the speed of the cars in Los Angeles. They certainly traveled faster than the vehicles in Swatow. She giggled as she thought of the battered busses, the handcarts, and the cars that had to dodge the bicycles and horses in Swatow. But still, would she ever get used to America?

After one week of lessons, both Florence and her father received a driver's license. That weekend Father drove the family to Paradise Valley, near San Diego, where he had a speaking engagement. From there, he had to go on to Arizona for a week of meetings, so it was up to Florence to drive the family back to Los Angeles. Later she was to say that this was the hardest task she had ever performed. Sonny sat in the back seat, but every time they came to a town he crouched down on the floor and stayed there until they reached the country again. He was sure they would be killed before they reached Grandfather and Grandmother Hansen's house in Glendale. In those days, cars couldn't travel much faster than forty miles an hour, but Florence averaged only about twenty-five! With all the stops it took to get through Los Angeles, it took eight hours to make the 140-mile trip. At her grandparents' house, they fell into bed, exhausted.

On September 1, 1929, the Nagels left Glendale and began the long-anticipated trip to PUC. Florence and her father took turns driving. When they finally drove up the narrow winding road to the college, Florence was eager to see their new home. She blinked twice when Father stopped the car. This couldn't be their new home—this was a doll house!

"Welcome home," he said. "Let's get the car unloaded."

Inside the tiny house was one bedroom, a living room, a kitchen, and a bathroom.

Mother took Florence by the hand. "Your room is out here," she said, leading her to a very small back porch. It had one single bed and a dresser in it. "Sonny will have to sleep in the living room until we get the woodshed remodeled for him."

Florence didn't know what to say. Their home in Wai Chow had been spacious. Even their house in Swatow had plenty of rooms. But this . . . well, if this was to be her home, she'd better make the best of it. After all, a missionary adapts, doesn't she? And what difference does it make? She was at college—that's what mattered the most.

At church on Sabbath in Irwin Hall, Father again met some old classmates. The college president, W. E. Nelson, was the first one to greet them. Two other schoolmates were on the faculty also. Dr. Homer Teasdale was head of the History Department, and Elder B. P. Hoffman was head of the Theology Department. Florence looked on with interest. This was a benefit of college she hadn't realized. It seems that college classmates meet each other all over the world.

Unfortunately Father couldn't spend much time renewing these friendships because he had accepted an appointment as the pastor of the Central Seventh-day Adventist Church in San Francisco. Grandmother Nagel would keep house for him and help him with the church activities. Her past experience as a Bible worker made her invaluable to the church. On weekends, he would come to PUC or the family would go down to San Francisco.

As the opening of school neared, Florence began to feel anxious. Yes, she was eager to begin. Yes, she was excited. But . . . what would school really be like? And what about all the other students? She had studied alone her whole life, and now there were four hundred students in the same school. At times, she felt panicky when she thought about it. Then she remembered her reason for being there: "I'm going back to China . . . and I must go!"

With the help of Aunt Letha, she enrolled in Accounting I, Bible Doctrines, English I, History of Missions, American History, Sewing I, Piano, and Chorus. It all sounded fascinating, but could she do it? Whenever she stopped to think about it, her heart pounded and her hands shook.

Then it came—the first day of classes! Florence slipped into a seat in her American History class; her toes didn't quite reach the floor. A few minutes later Dr. Teasdale entered the room and strolled up to the front desk. Florence looked around. So this was college. The room was filled with students, each with a pad of paper and a pencil, ready to take notes when the professor began. As Dr. Teasdale spoke, Florence began to relax her stiff shoulders. This wasn't going to be so bad after all.

Suddenly he paused and looked right at her. She froze.

"Miss Nagel," he said, "in what year was the first Continental Congress held?"

Florence opened her mouth, but no sound came out. The other students turned to look at her, some tittered. She took a deep breath and tried again. Still no sound. Then the room began to spin. Just as she felt herself slipping to the floor, everything went black.

CHAPTER TEN

The Co-op Schedule

Florence opened her eyes and found several students hovering over her. How absolutely embarrassing!

"I'm OK," she mumbled, struggling to get up. "I don't know what happened." She slipped back into her seat and looked at the professor. "Sorry, sir," she mumbled.

I must have been more scared than I realized, Florence thought.

That first question he asked was the last one Dr. Teasdale addressed to Florence for the rest of the semester!

In History of Missions class, Elder Hoffman assigned every student a project. Each needed to choose a country he or she would like to serve in if called to be a missionary. After doing research on that country, the student was to write a paper about it. Of course, Florence had decided long ago—China was her country. But . . . wouldn't it be a wonderful way to serve God if she could also help pioneer the work in . . . say, French Indo-China? So Florence researched French Indo-China and wrote a paper on that country. Anyway, Uncle Victor (who was also her classmate now) had chosen China.

The school year passed quickly. Sonny (or Sherman Jr. as he was now called) and Florence finally began to feel at home in this strange place called America. They enjoyed it much more than they had even anticipated, and living at home proved to be a blessing for them. For one thing, they didn't have to fight homesickness the way some new students did.

That first summer promised to be an exciting one for both brother and sister. Sherman Jr. signed on to work with a contractor building houses near Lake Tahoe.

Florence and Mother moved to San Francisco to live with Father for the summer. The highlight of the summer was to be the 1930 General Conference session, which would be held in the Civic Center Auditorium in San Francisco. Florence was excited at the thought of seeing old friends from far away. But before and after the session, she would be a colporteur in Chinatown. Florence began right away.

"Florence, where have you been all morning?" Father inquired one day when she came home for lunch.

"I've been downtown selling books," she replied.

Father smiled. "I'm proud of your enthusiasm for your work," he said. "But we need you at the registration desk in the Civic Center Auditorium to answer the phones and run errands. There's only a few days left before the General Conference starts, and some of the delegates are already arriving. There's a lot to do."

Florence felt that familiar sinking feeling. *Why must everything I want to do be interrupted?* she grumbled to herself. Then she remembered that every time she had to change her plans, God had made something good from each disappointment.

"OK, Papa," she finally agreed. "What do I do first?"

"Here are the car keys," he said, tossing them to her. "Go down to the pier and meet the delegates from Brazil. Harold Fisher just phoned and wondered what to do now that he and Mrs. Fisher have arrived. I told him you would be there in half an hour. Drive carefully, my dear."

Florence had met other ships during her year in America, so she found Harold and Edna Fisher easily and welcomed them to San Francisco. "And who is this young man with you?" she asked. "Father didn't say anything about a third person."

"This is Kenneth, our son," Mr. Fisher replied.

Once the Fishers had gone through customs and immigration, Florence drove them to the Civic Center, taking a few detours along the way so that they could see some of the sights of the city. She made sure that Kenneth knew about the youth meetings, and she talked to him about PUC and how great it was.

A few days later, she saw Kenneth again and asked how things were going for them.

"We're doing fine," he said. "By the way, you said you were a missionary from China. Did you meet Dr. Roger Paul at the Shanghai Adventist Sanitarium? He's my uncle."

Florence remembered Dr. Paul well. Then she asked where Kenneth went to school. He told her about his school in Brazil and said he also had to take some courses from the Fireside Correspondence School. He and Florence had a lot to talk about.

A few days later they met again. "Are you planning to come to PUC next school year?" Florence asked.

"No, I can't stay in America. I have to go back to Brazil with my parents and finish my high school there."

"Well, God bless you," Florence said. "Maybe we'll meet again someday. It was really nice to get acquainted with you." As she turned away, she couldn't help but wonder if their paths would ever cross again. She knew God worked in mysterious ways—and Kenneth seemed to be a nice boy.

★ ★ ★ ★ ★

The summer went by quickly as Florence sold books with her mother in Chinatown. She quickly became known in the neighborhood. Often, when Florence knocked on a door, the child who opened it would yell (in Chinese), "That woman who speaks Chinese is here!"

Every noon they spent resting at the home of Mrs. Susan Haskell Wilbur. It had been her husband, Edwin, who had rescued Mrs. Nagel and baby Florence from Wai Chow nineteen years earlier. Elder Wilbur had passed away in China. Now, here was his wife—in Chinatown, San Francisco, where she had opened a school to teach English and introduce the Chinese to the God she loved.

That summer, Florence was able to sell enough books to give her two scholarships to PUC! God was indeed good. The second school year went by even faster than the first. Florence graduated from the Bible Worker Course, but she looked forward to continuing at PUC until she received a bachelor's degree.

Late that summer, Father changed her plans yet again.

"Florence," he said, "I'm sorry, but you can't go back to college next semester. We are giving up the house in Angwin, and Mother is moving to stay with me down here in San Francisco. We can't afford to pay for both you and Sherman Jr. to stay in the college dormitory."

What a disappointment! But Florence remembered—God was working out the plans for her life.

When Professor Hoffman visited the Nagels, he asked why Florence wasn't returning to PUC the next month. Florence told him it was a matter of money and explained the situation.

A big grin spread across his face. "I have good news for you," he said. "You can come to PUC and be my secretary and reader. I just found out that the girl who worked for me last year is getting married and won't return. So if you work for me, you'll be able to earn enough to stay in the dormitory."

Professor Hoffman also persuaded Florence to take the theology course. This gave her the opportunity of helping in the services of the small churches in the valley below the college. And it was good training for a missionary wife, wasn't it?

During Christmas vacation, Florence and Sherman Jr. remained at school to work. One morning Florence was in the college kitchen fixing breakfast when "Ma" Spears, the food service director, walked in with three young men.

"Girls," she said, "I want to introduce you to three new students who have just arrived in the middle of the night. This is Al Cole from Japan, and that is John Hartman, and that one is Kenneth Fisher from Brazil."

Florence was happy to see Kenneth. "You did get to come!" she exclaimed. "I'm glad." Then her glance took in the others. "Let me know if there's anything I can do to help any of you. We missionaries have to stick together."

In the spring, about a week before graduation, Florence was fully occupied with exams, working, and planning the decorations for graduation ceremony. Then one day the registrar, Miss Olson, came to the office where Florence worked.

"I'm sorry, Florence," she began. "But in going over your records, I notice that you haven't taken History of the Reformation. There's no way you can graduate next week without having taken that class."

How disappointing! What should she do? Or more to the point, how was God planning to deal with this new circumstance?

Florence was soon offered a teaching job at an Adventist elementary school in Campbell, California. Was this the way God was leading her? If she took this job, she could take the course she needed by correspondence and go back to PUC to graduate with the Class of 1933. She accepted the position and enjoyed working with the children, but graduation weekend in June 1933, was the highlight of that school year for Florence.

What next? Finally, she agreed to teach another year, this time in Paradise, California. She loved the children, but slowly she was realizing that teaching was not her calling. It wasn't what God wanted her to do the rest of her life. After much prayer, she decided to go back to PUC. After all, God hadn't lined up a husband for her so far, so she'd take the Pre-Medical Course. Then she could go back to China as a lady doctor.

In September Florence began school again. Sherman Jr. was also finishing college that year as a pre-med student. By early spring, the pre-med students began to watch the mail for official letters of acceptance (or rejection) from the College of Medical Evangelists, now called Loma Linda University.

One day a student burst into the physics lab shouting that the letters had arrived. He waved a piece of paper and joyously exclaimed, "I'm accepted!" A dozen students raced out of the lab and headed for the post office. But not Florence.

"Sherman!" she called to her brother as he ran for the door. "Get my letter, please."

It was a long time before he returned. As soon as he entered the lab, she knew it was bad news for him.

"My GPA isn't high enough," he explained. "I'll have to take another class to get my GPA up and try for the second section. Here, read your letter."

Her hands trembled as she tore the flap off her envelope.

"You are accepted in the first section of 1935," the letter read. But in small handwriting at the bottom, a note was added. "The AMA [American Medical Association] will accept your oriental language credit. But we have no record that you have ever taken high school English literature. The AMA requires this. Please send us your grade."

Back in Swatow, Florence had enrolled in English Literature and had finished about two-thirds of the course when she had heard from PUC that she wouldn't need it. She had enough literature for the college's entrance requirements.

She wrote immediately to the Fireside Correspondence School, asking for advice. The director wrote by return mail, saying, "Finish five more lessons and take the final exam, and we will send your grade."

What a mess! She didn't even have those lessons or books anymore. But she knew where to start asking for help.

"Dear Lord," she prayed. "You are always prepared at the right moment to help me. You probably have this whole thing worked out already. So will You show me what to do?"

A few days later Florence stood in the college store telling her problem to a friend. Suddenly another classmate stepped up.

"Florence," he said, "I just heard what you said and I think I can help you. I took that course last summer, and I have all the lessons and books up in my room right now. You're welcome to borrow them."

What a miracle! Florence knew God was guiding her even in the smallest details. Not too many weeks later, the registrar congratulated her, saying, "I received a telegram from Fireside Correspondence School this morning. It says, 'NAGEL PASSED ENGLISH LITERATURE STOP GRADE FOLLOWS.'"

Studying medicine hadn't been in Florence's original plans when she left China, but she frequently quoted a verse she liked:

Disappointment, His appointment.
Change one letter, then you'll see
That His plan was best for thee.

On the day of Florence's first class in medical school, Mr. Fink, the registrar, met her at the door. "Miss Nagel," he told her, "you have been transferred to the second section which will start in one month. In the meantime, you may take the Physiotherapy Laboratory class with the girls of the first section. Also we have arranged for you to work in the kitchen."

This wasn't such bad news. This would mean that she and Sherman Jr. would be in the same class. That might be fun! She found out later that Kenneth Fisher was also to be in her class.

Florence completed the nursing course while at Pacific Union College in 1931.

These were the years of the Great Depression in the United States. Few students had money for tuition, and medical school was more expensive than college. To help with this problem, the College of Medical Evangelists arranged with many hospitals in southern California to give work to their students. The class of a hundred students was divided into two sections. Half began classes while the other half worked. To make this plan work, the two groups alternated between work and school every month. Doing this year around meant that the students had to study hard during their months "on." And they had to learn in six months of schooling what was usually done in a nine-month school term. Of course, outside reading requirements and papers could be done on the job.

Florence and Sherman Jr. enjoyed a friendly competition in their classes. They shared one set of textbooks. Florence often sneaked into his room very early in the morning to get Gray's Anatomy textbook so that she could study a little extra and get better scores on the quizzes that day. And there Sherman

Jr. sat, already studying. So they would cram together until class time.

For work during the months off from studies, Florence was sent to the Los Angeles County General Hospital to work as a night laboratory technician. At that time, this was the largest hospital under one roof west of the Mississippi River. She stayed in the girls' dormitory with a sophomore girl also from Loma Linda.

Florence worked from 2:30 P.M. to 11:30 P.M. six nights a week. Two junior medical students came in at six o'clock to work with her until she went home, then the other two were on call for the rest of the night. It was a strenuous program. Florence found herself slowly neglecting her personal morning devotions and Bible study. And during the months in the city, it was so easy to make excuses why she should not go to church. After all, she was exhausted, and no one would miss her anyway.

Occasionally she would go on a date to the mountains or the beach on Sabbath—just to get away from the grind, she told herself. It was easy to drift with the tide. Like many of her classmates, Florence was slowly, but surely, losing interest in going back to the mission field. It would be wonderful to have a large elegant home and plenty of money to spend someday when she finished this grueling program.

Toward the end of her freshman year, she became extremely ill. She was hospitalized for several weeks—measles and scarlet fever, the doctors said. She lost so much time from her studies that she had to drop out for a year and work until the next class caught up to her. About this time, the "co-op" system stopped. Students no longer studied one month and worked the next. The medical school went back to the nine-month school term. There was no way that both she and Sherman Jr. could be in medical school at the same time. There just wasn't that much tuition money in their family.

Florence looked at herself in the mirror. "OK," she said out loud. "What's next?"

CHAPTER ELEVEN

Keeping Promises

Florence applied to enter the already full medical technology course—and she was accepted. Now she could keep her night job and take the lab training during the day. What a miracle God performed! But right then, Florence wasn't looking for God's leading in her life. She was too busy working, studying, and pursuing an active social life. Before long she was engaged to be married to a junior medical student, a good-looking, brilliant young man. That year he held the honor of passing the first part of the National Board with the highest score in the nation! She was proud of him. His lack of interest in spiritual things bothered her a little, but not much. She was his chosen girl—that's what mattered.

Life went on smoothly for a while. The little voice of conscience spoke softly and was easily ignored. *Once we are married,* she told herself if she thought about it at all, *we'll go to church together. Things will be different then.*

Just a month before the wedding, Florence was driving back to Paradise Valley near San Diego from a delightful weekend visiting her fiancé in Glendale. It was after midnight, but she had to be on duty early the next morning. In places, the two-lane road going down the east side of Kellogg Hill was steep. Suddenly a slow-moving car loomed out of the darkness in front of her. Actually, she saw that it was two cars—one pushing the other. She pulled out to pass and met an oncoming car. Miraculously, she squeezed past. But as she pulled back into her lane, she hit loose gravel. The little Ford lost traction and veered off the pavement. Over and over it rolled and bounced down the hillside. The driver's door flew open just as the car came to a rocking halt.

The drivers of two cars she had just passed stopped to see if they could help. Florence heard some women screaming up on the road. Men climbed rapidly down the bank to see if she was still alive.

"Boy, am I lucky!" she exclaimed, crawling out of the pile of twisted metal. "I'm OK—no broken bones!"

One of the men looked her over. "You may not have any broken bones," he said, "but you'd better sit down. You're losing a lot of blood."

"Yeah, that's quite a gash you've got on your head, ma'am," added another man. "It's a miracle you're still alive, I'd say."

Florence felt something wet and looked down at her dress. In the light of the cars on the road above, she saw blood, lots of blood. Then her head began to throb.

Later, as she waited in the emergency room to be stitched up, something was niggling away at the corner of her mind. She couldn't quite put words to it.

Two days later in the quiet of her room in Paradise Valley, she sat in her favorite chair to think. Then she noticed her dust-covered Bible on the second shelf of the small table beside her. Idly she picked it up and dusted it off. Without thinking, she opened it to Psalm 34:7: "The angel of the Lord encampeth round about them that fear him, and delivereth them."

For hours she struggled with God, pleading for His blessing on the plans she'd made without Him. Then other verses popped into her mind, not verses from the Bible, but verses that she'd written herself on her sixteenth birthday—"I'm going back to China ... And I must go!" She was stunned to realize how far from God she had drifted. She had forgotten her promise to serve Him all the rest of her life.

As the sun rose, her head sank to her chest, and the tears finally flowed. "Dear Lord," she prayed. "You are so good to me, and I've treated You so badly. You saved my life in that accident; I know You did. Take my worthless life again and make it something beautiful to use for You. Father, forgive me. Keep me close to You now. Don't let me lose my vision of serving You."

Within the next few days, friends were shocked to learn that Florence had broken her engagement. When they questioned her, she only smiled and said, "God's in charge now."

Florence finished her training at Los Angeles County General Hospital as a medical technologist and went to work in Paradise Valley Sanitarium and Hospital. But always she kept her promise to God before her. In some ways, she felt like Moses who had wandered in the wilderness for forty years to prepare for his life's work. She hoped it wouldn't take her forty years, but she did feel as though she had endured hardships and tests to strengthen her faith.

Eventually Florence met another man, Ervin Winton, who was taking the pre-med course at La Sierra College. He was a kind, loving young man who shared her desire to serve God as a foreign missionary. He was a practical man, too. Before he enrolled in college, he had worked as a plumber and an electrician. These were good skills for a missionary to have, Florence told him. Their friendship deepened into love, and they planned a Thanksgiving wedding. After that, they expected to enter medical school together in the class that began on January 1, 1944, but the government had other plans.

On November 11, 1943, Uncle Sam sent Ervin an invitation to serve his country. Florence was used to her plans being changed, but she begged God to tell her what to do in this situation. She wanted to go back to medical school and actually finish it! In the meantime, Ervin was stationed in Denver, Colorado—and getting lonesome. He wrote, "Are you really planning to return to medical school? Why don't we get married, then you can come be with me."

She prayed earnestly for guidance. Then a letter came from Dr. Harold Shryock, Dean of the Loma Linda University Medical School:

> Dear Miss Nagel,
> We are sorry to inform you that we cannot accept your application for re-entrance into medical school this coming January. The United States Government has taken over the

medical school to train physicians for the army. Women will not be allowed in this program.

Well, this certainly answered her prayers. The way she wanted to go was closed, at least temporarily. So, on April 15, 1944, thirty-three-year-old Florence married Ervin Otis Winton in a beautiful military wedding in Camp Crowder, Neosho, Missouri. For the next year, they traveled coast to coast and down to the Gulf of Mexico at the army's expense. Florence became part of the Army Civil Service Corps, and at every base she worked in the hospital laboratory. Then without warning, Ervin was shipped overseas, and Florence was left alone in South Carolina.

She immediately requested a transfer to the West Coast, so she could be near her parents. When she got to California, she reported to the officer she was to work for. But she also presented him with a letter from Dr. Orlan Pratt, Chief of the White Memorial Hospital Laboratory, asking that Florence be released from civil service duty so she could teach in the hospital's Clinical Laboratory Training School. The request was granted. During the next eight years, Florence worked as a teacher and a technician, first for the White Memorial Hospital and then for Loma Linda Sanitarium and Hospital.

When Ervin's army days were over, he was finally able to return to La Sierra College to finish his pre-medical course. During the school year of 1946-47, he rode back and forth from Loma Linda to La Sierra with Rolland Howlett, who had been a missionary in French Indo-China and in Haiti.

In 1948, Ervin finally was able to enter medical school. Life was busy for the Wintons. And Florence was happy—almost. Two things bothered her peace. First, the rumors she was hearing about China. If the communists succeeded in taking over, China would be closed to missionaries. What would happen to all her friends there?

The second was even more personal. As the years passed, Florence realized that she and Ervin couldn't have children. To Florence, children made the family; she wanted children to complete their home.

On June 9, 1951, Florence was teaching summer school as usual when a student approached her at the end of class one Monday morning. "Mrs. Winton, didn't you say you wanted to adopt a baby during your husband's senior year in medical school?" he asked. "My wife works in the nursery, you know. And she told me there were three newborn babies up for adoption."

Immediately Florence called Ervin out of class, telling him to see the social worker at once.

Sorrowfully, he reported, "All three babies have been spoken for."

Just then the phone rang. It was the social worker.

"You're in luck!" she said. "The couple who had planned to adopt the little boy decided they couldn't do it at the moment. So he's yours, if you want him. He was born only a few hours ago, and he needs a mommy and daddy."

Together, Florence and Ervin rushed to the nursery. They fell in love immediately with the tiny bundle of wiggles.

"He's so beautiful!" Florence spoke in a hushed, awe-filled voice. She glowed as she looked up at Ervin. "Let's go get a layette and borrow a baby buggy, so William Lawrence Winton can have a bed!"

"And," Ervin added, "we need to tell your father that he is a grandpa now! How's that for a birthday present! He and his grandson will always share June 9 celebrations."

Not quite a year later, Ervin learned of another possible adoption. And on May 2, 1952, Ervin was allowed to assist the doctor in the delivery of their second baby. Florence paced anxiously in the nearby waiting room. Five minutes after the birth, Ervin rushed out to her.

"Our little girl is doing fine!" he sputtered with excitement.

A few minutes later, the nurse brought the baby to Florence. Mary Bernice Winton gazed sleepily at her new mommy. She was tiny and pink and perfect.

"Like a precious little bunny," Florence murmured softly. And Bunny she became.

Billy and Bunny thrived on the loving care their parents lavished on them. Florence prayed daily for guidance in raising these new lives. As she watched her precious babies, she smiled contentedly. Her family was now complete.

Those were busy years. Grandma and Grandpa Nagel lived nearby and often helped with the care of the babies while Florence kept teaching and Ervin finished medical school. In 1953, Florence marched with the other faculty members in her husband's graduation, but certainly none were prouder than she was.

Life was good for Florence. But she hadn't forgotten her promise to God. Before Ervin finished his intern year, they gave their names to the office that recruited doctors for foreign mission service. In a very short time, an invitation came from Thailand. Could they come right away?

Florence remembered her vow to return to China. Well, Thailand wasn't China. But missionaries weren't allowed in China anymore. And Thailand was next door to French Indo-China! Her interest rekindled for that area of the world. Ervin didn't need much persuading either. They sent word back right away that they were willing and eager to go.

First Ervin passed the State Boards. Then they had to get physicals, including a battery of injections against diseases rampant in Asia at that time. Household goods were sorted, and packing began. Finally an official-looking envelope arrived with their passports and visas. They were cleared. They could go. It was a joyous day!

At last the packing and the family visits were completed. Florence felt like her heart could burst, she was so happy. She was going back to—well, not China, but almost! To Asia, at least.

On June 9, 1953, Billy's second birthday, the Wintons went with a group of well-wishers to the Los Angeles International Airport. Florence looked out the window at the huge Pan American Air Clipper that would take them across the Pacific Ocean. She looked apprehensively at the two propeller engines on each wing. Could those little things really keep this enormous plane in the air? A thrill of anxiety ran down her spine. She was forty-two years old, and this would be her first plane ride! What would it be like to look down on the clouds?

More importantly, this was the first step in keeping her promise to return to China. She must return to China someday. But for now, it was time to board the plane for Bangkok.

And what a plane ride it was!

CHAPTER TWELVE

The Three-Star General

The constant roar of the airplane engines droned on for hours, lulling the Wintons to sleep. Suddenly the plane gave a huge jolt and made a noise that sounded suspiciously like a big cough. Florence jerked awake and looked outside. The engine closest to her window had stopped completely; the propeller wasn't turning!

Beyond the silent engine, she saw the plane's landing lights scanning the water far below. Try as she could, she saw nothing but water. Just before dawn as the sky was turning pink, the plane made an emergency landing on Midway Island. While the dead engine was being replaced, the passengers were allowed to get out, stretch their legs, and enjoy the fresh tropical air. Listening to some of the airport staff, they discovered that the plane just ahead of theirs had exploded in midair! Their pilot had his landing lights on looking for floating wreckage.

Florence was eager to get to Bangkok, but she wasn't all that eager to reboard the plane. She didn't like being so far above the earth, and she especially didn't like the takeoffs and landings. She relaxed again only when the plane stopped in Guam for refueling.

Manila was their first scheduled layover. They were met at the airport by missionaries and taken to a guest cottage on the mission compound south of Manila. They were just freshening up when someone knocked on the door. Florence opened it, and there stood

Joseph Hwang from Swatow! *Pastor* Joseph Hwang now, she discovered. Joseph was also the chaplain of the Manila Sanitarium. He took the Winton family to his home to meet his wife and children. In the next few days, he showed them all over the city.

When their plane left the airport in Manila bound for Hong Kong, the day was bright and sunny. Florence could hardly wait to get there. Even though she dreaded the plane flight, she was excited to be on the way. At last she would be able to introduce her husband to her old life and old friends. Once airborne, seat belts were unfastened, and people began to move about the aisles. Florence looked out the window to get the last glimpse of Manila and to see some of the other islands of the Philippines.

The pilot's voice spoke clearly over the speaker system: "Ladies and gentlemen, if you look out the left side of the plane, you will see the Santo Thomas Prison Camp down below. That's where many American missionaries and businessmen were interned during World War II."

Suddenly his tone changed, and he said sharply, "Ladies and gentlemen, please return to your seats immediately and fasten your seat belts. We are returning to Manila Airport for an emergency landing. As some of you can see, our Number 2 engine has caught fire. Please stay calm. Remember, we still have three engines."

As the airstrip came into view, ambulances and fire engines were coming rapidly from all directions.

Please, God, Florence prayed silently, *protect this plane. I know You didn't bring us all this way to serve You just to have us die before we get there. Help me to relax, Lord, and not be afraid.*

As the plane rushed toward the runway, Florence continued to beg God for the safety of the passengers and crew. And thanks to guardian angels and a skillful pilot, the plane made a smooth landing. But it was quite a while before Florence could swallow the huge lump in her throat. She thought longingly of the ships that had carried her to and from China in her childhood.

The next morning a Philippine Air Lines plane took the passengers to Hong Kong. It was a very pleasant, uneventful ride. Pastor and Mrs. J. P. Anderson, her old neighbors from Wai Chow, were waiting at the airport to meet them. Florence was proud to be able to introduce them to Ervin and the children. But what a mix-up! The Andersons had expected them to arrive the day before and had invited more than forty of Florence's old friends to their home for a Chinese dinner to celebrate the arrival. The guests had come. They had waited until the last plane from Manila had landed before they ate the banquet without the guests of honor.

Twenty-four years had passed since Florence Nagel had left China. She had expected to return within three years. But finally, Florence Winton had returned. She would have loved to stay right there in Hong Kong, renewing old friendships and showing her family the places she had loved. But duty called. And right then, duty meant Thailand.

A marvelous welcome awaited them in Bangkok. Though in usual mission style, the party wasn't only for the Wintons. It was actually a welcome/farewell gathering. Dr. and Mrs. Ralph Waddell, the founder of the Bangkok Sanitarium and Hospital, were leaving for the United States just as the Wintons arrived. Dr. Waddell and Florence had graduated from PUC in the same class.

Among those waiting to welcome the Wintons were Pastor and Mrs. Milne. He was now the president of the Thai Mission. They took the Wintons to live in their home during the few months the Wintons stayed in Bangkok.

While Ervin was introduced to the hospital and consulted about new techniques in practicing medicine, Florence was kept busy in another part of the hospital. The hospital administration asked her to help organize the laboratory and introduce more recent techniques. She was beginning to see why God had changed her plans from physician to lab technician.

Ervin Winton was on call one night when an important patient was admitted, but no one was told who he was. A Thai government limousine had brought him to the hospital with a heavy police escort. The patient had been in an auto accident on the way from the airport to town. Police were assigned to guard him the entire time he was in the hospital.

Dr. Winton checked him over and gave emergency care. He found that the man wasn't seriously injured, just badly shaken up from the accident. But he was expected to remain in the hospital for several days to fully recover.

The next morning, at her husband's request, Florence went with him to see his new patient. The man was amazed when this American lady walked in and began speaking Chinese to him. Florence was able to discover that he was a three-star general from the Nationalist Government in Taiwan. He had come for a special meeting with representatives from Burma and Thailand. Leaders from England, America, India, and Australia had also been invited to attend.

When General Chiang Kai-shek had moved his troops from China to Taiwan at the time the communists took over in 1950, some of his soldiers were unable to escape. They hid in the mountains of Burma and Thailand. Now the Taiwan government was requesting safe passage through Burma and Thailand so that the soldiers could come out of hiding and go to Taiwan.

As Florence visited with this man, he asked her where she learned to speak the Chinese language. She told him that she had been born in Asia and raised in Wai Chow. When he heard the name Wai Chow, his face beamed.

"I very well remember that place," he said. "I was a corporal at the time. After the city fell to Dr. Sun Yat-sen's troops, I and my soldiers came down the road from the east. We passed an American mission. The city gate was sandbagged, so we could not enter, but we were very thirsty. At the mission, two little white children drew water from their well for us to drink."

He paused abruptly and stared at Florence. "Could you possibly have been that little girl?"

Florence smiled and patted his hand. "Yes, I was that little girl."

The general rested his head back against the pillow with a happy sigh. "Twenty-eight years have passed," he said, "and we meet again. This is very pleasant for me. You will visit me again tomorrow? And then I will leave this bed. There is work to do."

The next day Florence went again with Ervin to see the general. He was all dressed, sitting on the edge of the bed waiting for them.

"I have a favor to humbly ask," he announced. "We need to have this meeting in a place that is private. A place where I can trust the people. Would it be possible for the meeting to be held in your esteemed living room?"

"Of course, you can," Dr. Winton assured him.

"I am in your debt," the general said, with a small bow to each of them. "Tomorrow I will present myself to your home to make the arrangements."

When he came, he asked Florence to be the hostess and to serve all the refreshments for his guests. No servants were to enter the meeting room. When the hour of the meeting came, Florence met each delegate at the door. She had never seen so many important people in one place in her whole life, but God kept her from being afraid or nervous. He must have brought her here for just such a purpose as this. At the end of the meeting, the general presented Florence with a red plaque in a gold frame expressing his appreciation for her kindness and hospitality.

When the general returned to Taiwan, he talked to Madam Chiang Kai-shek. She arranged with her husband to donate property to the Seventh-day Adventist Church in Taiwan in order to construct a new hospital. Ezra Longway (whom Florence had met in China) would oversee the construction.

As pleasant as it was in Bangkok, they could not stay there longer. They had been called to relieve Dr. Franklin Crider down on the island of Phuket in southern Thailand, where the church had a small mission hospital and clinic. It was furlough time for Dr. and Mrs. Crider.

The medical work in Phuket had begun because of the influence of one man, a tin mine owner named Tan Ching Ho. In his travels he had visited the Adventist hospitals in Bangkok and Penang. He sent a message to the mission in Bangkok asking the church to run a similar institution in his town—and offering to donate the building and the land.

Dr. Arthur Geschke, another PUC classmate, was chosen to go down to Phuket to start the hospital. Dr. and Mrs. Geschke had worked there for about two years when the Japanese invaded Thailand during World War II, and they had to evacuate on very short notice. A British gunboat steamed into the bay to rescue the missionaries, sending a launch as close to shore as possible. Even then, the Geschkes had to wade in water up to their armpits before they could be picked up. They left all the hospital equipment behind, praying for the Lord to somehow protect it.

On the gunboat, they found they were being taken to Singapore for safety. More foreigners were also rescued as the ship sailed down the west coast of Malaya. In Singapore, they met Rolland Howlett, acting treasurer of the Malayan Union Mission. He arranged for their travel by ship to the United States.

Back in Phuket, the nationals knew they had to do something to keep their little hospital from falling into enemy hands. So they took every piece of equipment and every piece of furniture and hid them in homes all over the island. Some of the larger items were stored in caves. After the war, Dr. and Mrs. Crider went down to Phuket to reopen the hospital. Imagine their surprise when the people came, each carrying a piece of hospital equipment or furniture. Larger pieces were loaded onto boats and brought around to the beach near the hospital and clinic. More than any words possibly could have, this action expressed the love the people felt for the hospital and its mission work.

Now the Wintons were going to work in Phuket for a year while the Criders went home to America for a much-needed furlough. The Criders had worked in Phuket for five full years without a break. It was a one-physician clinic with no days off.

At the airport, Florence got another lump in her throat when she looked at the small plane that would take them to their new home. But as the plane flew over the countryside, she saw small bamboo huts with thatched roofs clustered in small villages surrounded by rice fields, coconut palms, beetle nut palms, and papaya and banana groves. To her it was the most natural thing to see farmers using water buffalo to pull their plows. It was as though the years had rolled back and she was going home.

The three-hour flight ended with a short trip across the water, and at last Florence saw the little island of Phuket. From the sky, the beaches looked beautiful with white breakers washing up on the sand from the Indian Ocean. Rolling hills and several higher peaks rose from the center of the island. One ribbonlike road stretched the entire twenty-six miles of the island. Everything looked peaceful and inviting—like a real tropical island paradise.

The plane touched down in a cleared spot of jungle and bumped to a stop in front of the thatched hut that served as the air terminal. A small group of people stood beside the runway holding a big welcome banner. Tears came to Florence's eyes. Once again, joy surged through her heart. She knew she was doing God's will. These people were God's people, and they had won her heart already. When the Wintons stepped out of the plane into the hot sultry afternoon, the Criders were the first to welcome them. After many introductions and smiles and handshakes of warm welcome from the other hospital staff members, the Wintons were finally borne off to the Criders' home.

Florence looked around. Mrs. Crider kept house in a native-style hut in a poor section of town. A slaughterhouse was just down the street, and when the wind blew in that direction, the smells were almost unendurable. The city market was just behind the house. This also contributed a variety of odors. A stream ran along one side of the property. They were told it was snake infested, so Dr. Winton refused to let the children play outside. How happy Florence was to learn that the mission had provided a different place for them to live.

The house chosen for them was a brick structure with a high open basement. Because of the excessive heat, none of the walls went clear up to the ceiling; the last three feet were open lattice-work. No screens sheltered the windows, so flies, mosquitoes, lizards, centipedes, and snakes could get into the house easily. They soon learned that Phuket had a wide variety of poisonous snakes. Some even climbed trees. Florence and Ervin decided they would take great care when they moved in to see that the doors were kept closed at all times.

Just before moving day, the Criders' *amah* came to Florence. "Is it true, Missy?" she asked with a shudder. "Are you really going to move into the big house?"

"Yes, we are," Florence answered. "Is there a reason why we shouldn't?"

"Oh, Missy Winton, did no one tell you?"

"Tell me what?"

"That house—she is haunted. Nobody can live there."

CHAPTER THIRTEEN

One Year in Phuket

"My God is stronger than the evil spirits," Florence said, smiling at the little maid. "So, yes, we will live there."

She shared with Ervin, however, what the maid had said about the house being haunted. Before moving in, the family prayed together, dedicating their lives and their home to the Lord's work. They asked their heavenly Father to go before them and to cleanse their new home of evil spirits. And they were never once bothered by evil spirits during the whole year they occupied that house.

Living in the house, however, proved to be eye-opening for Florence in different ways. For instance, she learned she didn't need a dust pan when sweeping the floor; the cracks between the floorboards were wide enough for all the dirt to fall through! And there were dozens of holes in the walls. To bathe, Florence and her family had to go outside the house to a small walled area around the well. There they splashed water on themselves and rubbed a bar of soap over their bodies. Then they dipped the bucket back into the well for a pailful to pour over themselves to wash away the soap. There was no place to heat water.

The kitchen consisted of three clay charcoal stoves in a building attached to the house. And of course, there was no running water there either.

With the land getting two hundred inches of annual rainfall, the humidity was exceptionally high. Sometimes the entire town flooded after only a few hours of heavy tropical rain. Florence understood, more and more, the reason for the high open basement.

One day when it wasn't raining, she smiled as she watched little three-year-old Billy and two-year-old Bunny entertaining themselves in the yard. They seemed to be having a lot of fun. Then Florence looked more closely—and gasped. A cold shiver ran down her spine. The children were teasing a small cobra! They squealed with delight when the snake hissed at them. Moving slowly and praying hard, Florence got the children's attention without startling them, and called them to come to her. Then while Florence sat in the doorway with one shaking arm around each child, a servant killed the snake.

Florence also had work to do at the hospital and clinic, so God led her to a sweet Chinese lady who came to be the *amah* for Bunny and Billy. Every afternoon, following their naps, the *amah* dressed up the children and took them for a walk—frequently ending up at the hospital to see their mother. The little white children were as much of a curiosity to the residents of Phuket as Florence and Sonny had been years before in China.

Florence's first task outside her home was to reorganize the medical laboratory in the hospital and to teach the man who worked there how to run tests on the new equipment she had brought from America. He was an apt learner, so soon she was free to do other things.

Next she turned her attention to the business office. It appeared that a lot of the income was slipping out the back door. Using different methods, she was able to locate the source of the pilfering and the person responsible. That person was asked to resign. Then Florence tackled the problem of disappearing hospital linen. This mystery was cleared up when a staff member appeared unexpectedly at the home of the woman who did the hospital's washing. This laundry worker had been tearing the hospital sheets into hand-towel-sized pieces and using them as diapers for her babies.

A big problem at the hospital was the lack of running water and flush toilets. As soon as Dr. Winton finished plumbing his home, he immediately turned his attention to the clinic and hospital. In his "free" time he began the renovation. What a curiosity the toilets were! And the patients enjoyed the showers so much that the hospital patronage increased! So the next project was to add more patient rooms to the hospital. A larger patient load required more nursing help. Things were happening fast.

Up to this time, no Protestant church services had been held on the island. Two Catholic priests had a small meeting place and a school, but that was all. Besides the doctor's family, only three other people on the hospital staff were Adventists. Before the Wintons came, the small group of believers had met either in a private home or out on the beach. So now, with things going well at the hospital, Florence turned her attention to the church services.

"Ervin," Florence began one day, "let's have a real church service. If you preach, maybe even some of your patients will come."

"Oh, no!" he said, shaking his head. "I'm not a preacher; you know that. I'm a doctor."

Florence was undaunted. "What if I wrote out the sermon? Would you do it then?"

"Well . . ."

"Good! Actually this is a good idea because then the interpreter will be able to look over the material first. Now all we need to do is find an interpreter."

Finding an interpreter, however, proved to be a problem. Edward and Miriam Lim, the one Adventist family, were Chinese and couldn't translate into Thai. The only Thai Christian spoke very limited English. The only qualified interpreter they could find didn't have a knowledge of the Bible. But having the material ahead of time made it possible, and at last the Adventists had a church service to attend regularly.

Then Florence organized a Sabbath School. With Bunny and Billy and the Lims' three children, there were five children in the kindergarten division each week. It grew rapidly. Next Florence decided to start a branch Sabbath School.

Because of the tin mines on Phuket, a number of young English-speaking families, mostly from Australia and England, lived in the area. Young families meant lots of children. When Florence asked the mothers if they would be interested in having a Sunday School for the children, they responded enthusiastically. Some wealthy English-speaking Chinese also wished to send their children. So every Sunday morning Florence conducted a branch Sabbath School in her home. On Sunday mornings, private chauffeurs would drive up, bringing the children. Each brought a little chair to sit on, and before long the room was filled to overflowing every week.

All week long, Florence planned for the branch Sabbath School. Every Saturday night she hung pictures and decorated her living room for the children. Then Sunday afternoon, she took down all the decorations. This became such a chore that she finally decided to leave the things up all the time. At first, guests were a bit startled at the décor—until she explained her project. As a result, many people helped her with gifts and contributions.

Florence longed to do something also for the hospital patients. She decided to have a story time on Friday evenings. She had brought many Bible slides with her to Thailand; they were gifts from evangelists in America. She arranged some of these to illustrate simple Bible stories. One Friday evening during visiting hours, she set up a projector and a screen in the hospital waiting room.

When everything was all set, she unfolded her small organ (another donation from America) and began to play. Ambulatory patients had already been invited to come down and see the pictures and hear the music. Bunny and Billy stood beside the organ and sang their Sabbath School songs. Patients, staff members, and visitors alike crowded near to hear the children and see what the doctor's wife was going to show on the screen. The front door stood open, so as soon as the slides began, people walking past in the street changed course and slipped in the door to watch and listen. Within minutes, the place was packed. People stood in the entrance and sat on the stairs, all trying to hear the Bible stories. Those who couldn't get in vowed to come earlier the next week so that they could see the pictures too.

Mrs. Fu, a tuberculosis patient, stayed in the hospital for several months. The Bible stories she heard on Friday nights caught her interest and spoke to her heart. When her family came to visit her from their village, a two-hour walk away, she told them what she'd heard. One day she told her husband to take down the ancestral shrine at home; they must now worship only the God of heaven.

When the time came for Mrs. Fu to be released from the hospital, she begged for someone to come to her village to teach her and her neighbors about the living God. So another branch Sabbath School was planned. It would meet every Sabbath afternoon at four o'clock in Mr. Fu's tailor shop on the main street of the village. Edward Lim offered to be the teacher. He spoke only Chinese and English, however, so he needed an interpreter. A businessman in the village volunteered to translate the message into Thai. So everything was set.

The day for the first branch Sabbath School finally arrived— but would anyone come to a tailor shop to listen to stories about the God of heaven? The answer was soon apparent. As quickly as Florence set up her folding organ and began to play, the people crowded into the shop. Mr. Lim used the Sabbath School picture roll to tell simple Bible stories. Sabbath after Sabbath the interest grew. Even the man who translated became so interested that he wanted more studies.

One elderly gentleman came every time and sat in the front row. One afternoon he brought a beautiful Chinese Bible with him. It was brightly colored and in perfect condition.

"Is this the revered Book you are speaking from?" he asked Edward.

"Grandfather!" Edward exclaimed in surprise, using the usual term of respect. "Where did you get such a beautiful copy of the Holy Bible?"

"Forty years ago when I left China, a friend presented me with this Book as a farewell gift. He advised me to read it carefully." The old man sighed. "I knew it was a Christian book, so I refused to read it. It has been wrapped up in my trunk all these years. Now I will go home and read it."

And that's just what he did. Later his son reported, "Father will not put that Book up even to eat! He reads it all the time."

Mr. Fu also became convinced Edward spoke the truth. He, too, wanted to learn more about the living God. The Fus had a lovely daughter still living at home. When her admirer came to call, Mr. and Mrs. Fu talked to him about the Bible.

The branch Sabbath Schools that Florence held on the island of Phuket in southern Thailand ended with evangelistic meetings and a baptism in the ocean. Mr. Fu (first on the left, front row), whose tailor shop was the location for one of the branch Sabbath Schools, was among those baptized.

One day Mrs. Fu told him, "Son, if you wish to marry our daughter, you must become a Christian. We now worship the God of heaven." Before long, the young man asked for Bible studies.

Requests for branch Sabbath Schools now grew so fast that the five church members couldn't keep up with them. They notified the Mission Office in Bangkok that they needed help. First a pastor came to study with those who were most interested. Then more and more people from surrounding villages asked for a teacher.

Finally the Mission headquarters sent an evangelist to hold meetings so that a great many people could learn at the same time. They rented the local theater across the street from the Buddhist temple, and people came—many, many people came.

What a thrill it was to attend that first baptism down by the ocean! One of the first to be baptized was the old man with the beautiful Bible. When Mr. Fu was baptized, people noticed that shortly after he came up from the water, he walked out on the rocks, away from the group gathered on the shore. Then they saw him throw something into the water.

When he returned to the shore, the pastor asked, "Brother, what did you do out there?"

"Oh, Pastor," Mr. Fu replied, "God says He casts our sins into the bottom of the sea. And you see, I threw away the clothes that belonged to the old man of sin. Now I am a new creature. I have made a new shirt and trousers to wear, and I want to follow Jesus for the rest of my life."

★ ★ ★ ★ ★

As Christmas drew near, Florence was feeling a little lonely. She wanted to make a nice celebration for her children on this tropical island, but she wasn't sure what to do. First, she decided to invite the hospital staff to a party in her home. She could decorate for Christmas and serve refreshments. But that didn't seem like enough for the children. Children should have grandparents and aunts and uncles at Christmastime.

Then a letter arrived from Mrs. Milne in Bangkok. "I will be arriving Christmas morning to spend a few days with you," she wrote.

Nothing but the coming of her own mother could have brought Florence more joy! Billy and Bunny squealed and jumped up and down when they heard the news. They immediately began planning a gift for "Grandma" Milne. Needless to say, Christmas that year was a happy time.

Phuket was a wonderful place to live. The beaches were perfect for swimming, and it was relaxing to spend an hour in the cool water after a busy day at work. Occasionally the family combed the coral reef looking for unusual shells. Once in a while, the clinic would close at noon, and the staff enjoyed a picnic together on the beach. These occasions brought the employees closer together and strengthened their dedication to the hospital.

The year in Phuket passed swiftly. Florence and her family loved the island, but soon the Criders would return—and the Wintons would leave.

As Florence began packing up her household, she prayed often. *Where are we to go, Lord?* she asked. *It's so beautiful here. Can't we stay? The hospital is busy enough now to use two doctors, isn't it? Oh, Lord, I really don't want to leave. Unless . . . Could You maybe open up China so that we could go there?*

Then a telegram arrived from the Mission headquarters in Singapore that changed her whole outlook. Florence beamed when Ervin read her the telegram. It said, WOULD YOU GO TO SAIGON STOP NEED MEDICAL WORK STARTED THERE.

Saigon! Saigon was in Vietnam, the brand-new country that used to be part of French Indo-China! If she couldn't go to China, and she couldn't stay here in Phuket, Vietnam was the one place above all others in the world she most wanted to go to. Her enthusiasm was infectious, and before long Ervin wired a reply: They would happily accept the new assignment.

As they had a year earlier, a group congregated at the Phuket airport—this time to greet the Criders as they returned. They held up a big welcome banner—just as they had when the Wintons arrived. But the hospital staff had increased so much during that year that the group was three times as large.

The next day, Florence and her family sadly said farewell to all the friends and hospital workers they were leaving. She loved them all so much. But real joy was found in doing God's bidding, and they were bidden to Saigon.

Completing the paperwork and arranging for visas for Vietnam took a long time, so first the Wintons headed south to Singapore, stopping on the way to help out in the hospital on the island of Penang, a tropical paradise off the west coast of Malaya. Dr. Harry Miller was relieving the regular doctor at the hospital there. Florence had heard many stories about the well-known "China Doctor," but she had never met him—at least not since she was an infant. Florence and Ervin worked with Dr. Miller for a few days before they boarded the train for Singapore.

The train was a novelty for Bunny and Billy. They were delighted to sleep on the funny little shelves that folded down from the wall. Then early one morning the porter tapped on their door and called, "Up! Up! We coming into Singapore soon."

Florence waited eagerly for her first glimpse of Singapore. Perhaps she expected a Chinese city that would remind her of Wai Chow or Swatow. But what she saw was British—at least on the surface. Stores held every modern convenience; on every hand beautiful clothes and wonderful works of art tempted buyers. But Florence and Ervin were more interested in learning about the proposed hospital project in Saigon. They were eager to hear all the plans. But there were no plans; what they heard was history.

"Fourteen years ago," began John Nerness, the Union president, "there was a sea captain by the name of Hall. He was so impressed with the Adventist medical work he had seen in many places throughout Asia that he donated forty-five hundred U.S. dollars to open up the medical work in French Indo-China. There was a problem, though. You see, this was *French* Indo-China. And no physician could work there unless he was either French or a Vietnamese who had trained in France. The mission couldn't find a doctor who met these qualifications. So in Saigon, there is only a small maternity hospital in Cholon, the Chinese part of town. It was opened by Marthe Bentz, an Adventist missionary from France.

"But now French rule is over in Vietnam," Pastor Nerness continued. "We are so grateful that you have accepted the challenge of beginning a real hospital in Saigon. But you need to know that we haven't much money earmarked for use there. You will need to purchase supplies and equipment here in Singapore to take with you. You won't be able to find much when you get there." He paused and looked down at the papers lying on his desk. Then with an almost embarrassed expression on his face, he said, "All we can give you at this moment is two thousand dollars. I'm sorry about that, but do what you can with it. God will have to supply the rest."

CHAPTER FOURTEEN

A Small Beginning

Two thousand dollars! How in the world could anyone hope to equip a whole hospital with only two thousand dollars? A single piece of good equipment might cost ten times that amount! But Florence and her husband were missionaries, and Dr. Winton was a master at repairing broken things. So they set out to scour Singapore for inexpensive medical equipment and supplies.

The shopping spree proved mildly successful. Their purchases filled only seven medium-sized boxes—but it was a start.

During the three-day wait until their ship arrived from France, they were well entertained by many of Florence's acquaintances from childhood. Lucy Chan, who had been one of Florence's best friends in Wai Chow, now lived in Singapore. She and Florence had a great time bringing each other up-to-date on what had happened through the years.

Another good friend, Jean Liu, had been the girls' dean at Mrs. Nagel's school in Wai Chow. Now she worked at Youngberg Memorial Hospital in Singapore. Florence was especially interested in hearing Jean's stories of the war years in China. Jean had served in the United States Army, in the blood bank, during World War II. She had been through some terrible bombing raids in Chungking. Now she was back at work in one of the mission hospitals. Her husband was taking the laboratory technician's course, and her son

A Small Beginning

Henry was already a lab technician. Jean's daughter, Betty, was in the United States attending school at Pacific Union College. The years had passed so quickly, Florence had a hard time believing that Jean had grown children already!

Florence and her family crowded a lot of activity into those last three days in Singapore. They even found time to visit the Far Eastern Division headquarters on its compound about five miles away on Thomson Road. Far Eastern Academy had been moved from Shanghai to Hong Kong to Singapore and now occupied the back half of the Division compound.

Thaipusam, a Hindu religious celebration, was taking place in the temples along Serangoon Road. During this celebration, good Hindus took part in purification rites in order to prepare for the fire-walking ceremony and for the body piercing and the ritual walk from one temple to another. All this was done to win favors from the gods.

Along with other tourists, Florence and Ervin watched men walk through a long bed of hot coals. At the end of the fire pit a strategically placed trough of cows' milk cooled the burning feet.

Later, in another temple courtyard, the Wintons watched while a priest chanted into the ear of a worshiper. The chant continued until the worshiper's eyes grew glassy—evidence that the man was in a deep trance. Then began the body piercing. The man's tongue was stretched out, and a small knife blade was pushed through it so that his tongue couldn't retract into his mouth. Then a *kavate,* a huge structure made of wire and peacock feathers, was lowered onto his shoulders, and slim, pointed poles protruding downward from the *kavate* were pushed into the flesh of the man's back and chest to support the structure.

Florence saw another man standing on strange shoes. Many nails stuck up through the soles of the shoes, and the man was standing on these sharp nails. The flesh of his back and chest was pierced with dozens of wire hooks, each with a lime hanging from it.

The men participating in these rituals had fallen into deep trances and seemed to have no sense of pain—or of direction. When each participant was ready, he was guided to the street by a friend who stayed with him for the mile-long walk to the next temple.

The Wintons were glad to leave these scenes behind them. They thanked God for His unconditional love, a love that doesn't demand meaningless and physically painful ceremonies before a person can be saved. They rejoiced in a Savior whom they delighted to serve.

After sundown on Sabbath, friends took the Winton family to the dock to board the SS *Marseilles,* scheduled to weigh anchor for Saigon at midnight. Florence had expected a small coastal liner, but the SS *Marseilles* turned out to be France's largest luxury liner. The gorgeous ship filled Florence with pleasant memories of other ocean voyages. Even traveling second class didn't blight her enjoyment. Because very few passengers were traveling second class, Bunny and Billy had the decks largely to themselves to run and play. Fortunately, the South China Sea remained calm throughout the voyage.

On the morning of the third day, the ship entered the mouth of the Saigon River. Small villages surrounded by rice paddies stretched as far as the eye could see on both sides of the river. Sometimes the river curved so sharply that Florence expected the ship to get stuck, but it continued. They passed many freighters flying the American flag; these ships were tied up along the river bank, waiting to be unloaded. They were filled with food and supplies for the million or more refugees who had flooded into Saigon from North Vietnam during the long war for independence from France. Florence had heard that many of these refugees lived on the sidewalks of the capital city in appallingly unhealthful conditions.

Late in the afternoon, Florence could see the tall buildings of Saigon and the steeples of its churches in the distance. From the ship it looked just like the pictures of Paris—without the Eiffel Tower!

As the ship pulled into the dock, Billy yelled, "Look, Mama! See all the soldiers down there? And look at the band! Is it for us, do you think?"

For more than an hour after the SS *Marseilles* docked, the passengers waited. No one was allowed to leave the ship. Then a small elderly man carrying only a black hat started down the gangplank. He was escorted by a solicitous French officer.

Florence heard people asking each other: "Who is he?" "He must be important!" Then the soldiers on the dock snapped to attention, and the band began to play. When a member of the ship's crew walked by, the passengers questioned him about the small man.

"That man?" the steward asked. "Oh, that's the king of Laos. He has lived in Europe for many years, exiled from his people. Now he is going home."

No wonder he's getting a royal welcome! Florence thought. *But who's to welcome us?*

She had noticed a group of people crowded into the shade of a large tamarind tree just beyond the wharf. Two individuals stood out in the group of Vietnamese. One was a tall, very blond man. Even from this distance he seemed impatient for the ceremonies to be over. Florence figured he was American. The lady beside him looked American, too — or at least European. Could they be the Mission director, Pastor Elton Wallace, and his wife, Evelyn?

She had guessed correctly. This young minister had been trying to open up much-needed medical work in Vietnam. This was an exciting day for him: The doctor had arrived! Pastor Wallace and his wife along with the national workers had waited all afternoon under the tamarind tree to give the Wintons their very own royal welcome.

While the workers chattered their happy welcome, Florence heard someone behind her say, "Lotus Blossom? Do you remember me? I'm Lillian."

Florence spun around and stared in open-mouthed surprise. "Of course I remember you!" she cried, hugging Lillian. "You've grown up as much as I have, but how could I forget all the fun we had on the compound in Wai Chow?"

Lillian was the third daughter of Ah Tien and Ah Vu. Now she was married to Paul Hung, the pastor of the Chinese church in the area of Saigon where most of the refugees from China lived. Lillian was helping in the small maternity clinic operated by the church— the only medical mission work currently in the city.

Lillian and Florence couldn't visit long, however. The Wintons' baggage must go through customs. And the wonderful people who had waited in the hot, sultry sun for hours for their ship to arrive needed to go home and rest.

The customs officers took exception to the boxes of American and British medicines they were bringing in, as well as the seven boxes of hospital equipment from Singapore. They confiscated all of it!

How could Florence and her husband open a hospital with absolutely no supplies at all? It would take many months of negotiating with the customs authorities—and one miracle—before the equipment and supplies were finally released.

Pastor and Mrs. Wallace drove the Wintons to their temporary lodgings, telling them about the city of Saigon as they traveled. The nine square blocks by the waterfront gave the impression of a French city. Even the street names were French. The signs on the buildings could easily be read—though they made no sense to Florence. They weren't Chinese, English, or French. Through the years, the French Catholic priests had developed Roman equivalents for the old Chinese characters brought from China by the ancestors of the local people. The priests wrote out everything using this new alphabet and taught the new writing in their schools. Fortunately for Florence, Vietnamese still retained enough similarities with Chinese that she was able to follow sermons in church, though she could never translate it.

Away from the center of town, the scenery changed. The French architecture and big businesses were left behind. The shops were small, and families lived above their businesses. The smell of familiar Chinese spices filled the air. But the traffic was horrendous. Bicycles, motor scooters, and a thousand pedestrians vied for space in the street with the cyclo, a strange vehicle that had a cab pushed by either a man, a motorcycle, or a bicycle. There were no sidewalks. Scattered through this busy scene was a smattering of private automobiles and taxis, each driver honking continuously. To Florence the congestion and noise were worse than Bangkok.

Florence was impatient to see the building where the hospital would be. At a main intersection of two busy streets, Pastor Wallace pointed to a small, two-story building. "There it is!" he said proudly.

"Oh, no!" Florence blurted out. "That doesn't look big enough even for a home, let alone a hospital!"

Elton Wallace smiled ruefully. "Wait until you get a better look at it," he said. "Actually, that building used to be our Mission headquarters. We moved all our offices to some very cramped quarters in the Signs Press building just so you could have the use of this place."

Elton Wallace had worked very hard for many months, visiting officials and convincing them of the importance of allowing the Mission to operate a hospital. With the French no longer in control, a much more pro-American attitude existed in the government, and finally his petition was granted. By ministerial decree an American physician was granted permission to practice medicine, but only within the limits of the hospital. Florence realized how important this decree was, and she also realized what Elton was too humble to say: His own pleasant, friendly personality, plus his knowledge of both the French and Vietnamese languages and his keen sense of diplomacy—along with God's help—had won the favor of the government officials.

Much to Florence's surprise, local Adventists gave a reception in the Wintons' honor that first evening. It took place in the large room on the second floor of the old Mission headquarters—or the new hospital—depending how you looked at it. All of the Mission workers and their families attended, as well as many church members. The highlight was a large cake, decorated on top with a map of Vietnam made out of frosting. Where the dot for Saigon should have been on the map, a large red cross marked the spot where the hospital would be located. Dr. Winton was given a knife and asked to make the first cut. As he lifted the knife, someone called out, "Please, Doctor, do not cut it east to west; we are already divided there!"

When the reception was over, the Wintons were taken on a tour of the building. The first two floors each had one large room and one small room. The third floor was a single large room without a ceiling—just the rafters and pointed roof overhead. These floors were connected by a circular cement stairway from top to bottom. A small entrance hall and an open porch gave access to the building.

The building was situated on a corner of a very busy intersection. One street led downtown, while another went to a large French military camp. A third went to the airport, and the fourth was the main thoroughfare leading to Route 1 east to Hanoi. A little booth stood in the middle of the intersection for the policeman who directed traffic. The noise was deafening—certainly not an ideal place for a hospital!

But in the mission field, one takes what one gets, Florence told herself, *and one makes the best of it. Besides, everything must begin small.*

That night, Ervin and Florence worked far into the night, laying out possible floor plans for the hospital. They knew that the next day the Union president, Elder John Nerness, and the treasurer, Mr. Cleveland, would be coming from Singapore to look at their plans and make decisions about the new hospital. The plans must be ready to be authorized at this first board meeting.

After breakfast the next morning, Florence sought out the Mission director, Elton Wallace. "By any chance, do you have a carpenter's tape and a box of colored chalk?" she asked.

"I sure do," he replied. "If you need them, I'll get them for you."

Ervin, Florence, and Elton went to the proposed hospital building, and the Wintons laid out the plans they had made the night before. Then using the chalk, the three of them drew on the floor the placement of each piece of equipment, each item of furniture, and each wall they hoped to have.

The men from Singapore arrived on schedule, and on the afternoon of October 26, 1954, the first board meeting of the new hospital convened. After prayer and a few remarks, the business began. The committee voted to accept the kind offer of the Vietnam Mission to use its office building for the hospital. The next item on the agenda was the official appointment of Dr. Winton as the medical director and Florence as the business manager and secretary of the new hospital. Then they turned to the matter of a name for the new facility. Florence urged the committee to include the name of the church in whatever title they gave to the new hospital.

"How about calling it Saigon Adventist Hospital?" she suggested. The committee liked the name, and it was officially adopted.

Then the committee needed to talk about money. The main question being: Where would the money come from to renovate and operate the facility? The building had to be remodeled, equipped, and staffed before it could be opened. Florence and Ervin soon learned that the forty-five hundred U.S. dollars that Captain Hall had donated for the hospital had been "borrowed" to begin the Bangkok hospital. The funds had never been replaced. And the Bangkok hospital still wasn't financially stable enough to begin paying back the money. There was no money for a hospital in Vietnam! In fact, the new hospital was already two thousand dollars in the red for the equipment that was still down on the docks with the other boxes of supplies. Florence knew it could also cost a lot of money to pay the customs duties when they were finally allowed to take the supplies—if they were ever allowed to. In addition, half of the cost to bring the Winton family to Saigon had been charged to the maternity clinic, as had their salaries since they had left Thailand.

Finally Pastor Nerness spoke up, "We do have some hope to offer. All of the Harvest Ingathering funds for this year may be used for remodeling this building. But this means that nothing can be done until the money comes in."

In this climate, the plans for remodeling the building were presented! Florence and Ervin gave the committee a guided tour of the imaginary institution with its chalked fixtures. Everyone agreed that the plans were reasonable. Then the committee voted on a local board of directors for the hospital. Elton Wallace would serve as chairman, and Florence would be the secretary of the board. The committee also voted to go ahead with remodeling the first floor so that the outpatient department could be opened as soon as possible. In this way, cash would begin to come in.

Harvest Ingathering began the very next month. Businesses and people who lived around the proposed hospital grew excited about the project, and the donations began to roll in. But not every donation was in the form of cash. One company donated a safe, another a typewriter and calculator. Some gave furniture. Florence had brought her own microscope; other laboratory equipment had been donated by friends in America. Miraculously these items had escaped confiscation by the customs officials; the hospital would be able to do some lab tests at least!

Florence hired a carpenter right away and put him to work on the remodeling. Ervin spent his time fixing the plumbing and electricity; Florence set up an accounting system and prepared the many forms that would be needed. These she sent to the press to be printed. She also interviewed prospective workers.

There was so much work to do. Too much. Day after day Florence worked long, hard hours; each night she went home too exhausted even to talk to her children. The task began to seem overwhelming.

"Lord, I can't do this anymore," she prayed one day. "It's too much. What am I going to do? If You'd provide the money, I'd take my family home to America right now and forget this whole thing!"

It soon became apparent to everyone that happy, enthusiastic Florence was discouraged and ready to quit.

CHAPTER FIFTEEN

Miracles, Miracles!

"Florence," Elton Wallace said one morning, "you've been working nonstop since you arrived in Saigon. It's time for a break. The Mission has voted to send you and your family to Hong Kong for a month's vacation."

A telegram went immediately to Pastor J. P. Anderson in Hong Kong asking if an apartment were available for occupancy. The reply arrived the next morning. Yes, an apartment was available, and the Wintons were most welcome to use it. Tickets and visas were obtained that afternoon, and the following day the family boarded an Air Vietnam plane bound for Hong Kong. Pastor and Mrs. Anderson met them at the airport.

The cold wintry weather of Hong Kong was a marked change from Vietnam, and after a few days, Florence's energy began to return. She took long walks to the old cemetery, looking at the graves of the church pioneers and remembering a poem she had written on her sixteenth birthday—one she had almost forgotten—"I'm going back to China . . . And I must go!" She remembered her solemn promise to return to help her friends in China. Well, Vietnam wasn't China, but many of the people were Chinese.

"Dear Father," she prayed, "forgive me for not remembering You sent me to Saigon and will sustain me and guide me. I was

127

trying to rely on myself, and it didn't work. I am so ashamed, Lord. Help me to get back the missionary zeal I once had, and keep me close to You."

In Hong Kong, the Wintons spent time together as a family. Florence and Ervin took the children on outings and played with them, trying to regain some of the closeness they had lost in the mountain of work in Saigon. Once Florence finally regained her vision, she grew eager to return to Saigon. After all, there was a hospital to open.

Soon after she returned to Saigon, Florence began a class in medical English for the first group of workers chosen to staff the new facility. She knew very little Vietnamese, and she had no medical dictionary to help her. So she simply held up a thermometer and spoke slowly in English: *ther-mom-me-ter*. The students repeated this word over and over. Then she picked up the next object and carefully repeated its name in English. Little by little, the new staff learned the English names of many items commonly used in the hospital.

As Florence got acquainted with each of the workers, their future role in the hospital became clear to her. She often had to stop and bow her head in awe at the miracles she saw God performing as she put together the personnel for the hospital staff. Whatever the position needing to be filled, it seemed that God came up with the perfect person.

Even Florence's childhood friend Lillian Hung came to work for the new hospital. For nearly a year, she was the only outpatient nurse in the hospital. At the Hungs' request, the Mission found another pastor for the Chinese church, so Lillian's husband could come to work in the hospital laboratory. He soon became an efficient laboratory technician.

On May 22, 1955, the outpatient department of the new Saigon Adventist Hospital opened for business—with little equipment and few medicines.

The very first patient was a small French baby with pneumonia. Like many of the patients to follow, his mother had taken him to the local doctors until it became apparent that he wasn't recovering. He was thin and gaunt, and he breathed in loud, raspy, painful

The original Saigon Adventist Hospital, opened May 22, 1955.

gasps. The Wintons prayed earnestly over this little baby. It was of utmost importance to the success and reputation of the hospital that it not lose its first patient! *Why, oh why,* thought Florence, *didn't the hospital have the inpatient services available yet so it could take proper care of him!* But with prayer and care, the baby began to improve. The whole staff breathed a thankful sigh when the mother returned a few days later carrying a happy, well baby.

Several weeks later, a man banged on the Wintons' door in the middle of the night. "Please come, Doctor," he begged. "My wife is very sick. She needs help badly."

The Wintons had already learned that Vietnamese physicians wouldn't take night calls, so Dr. Winton dragged himself out of bed to attend to the lady. God helped him heal her quickly. And this opened the way for the miracle they so badly needed.

While tending to the patient, Dr. Winton had noticed her husband's uniform—the uniform of a government customs agent. So when her husband came back to see him, Dr. Winton was ready.

"Doctor, I am so grateful that you made my wife well," the husband said. "You even came in the middle of the night. I would like to do something for the hospital. What do you need?"

"We do have a problem you might be able to help us with," Dr. Winton said. "In the customs warehouse is a pile of boxes containing our medicines and hospital equipment. We need those boxes badly to care for patients at the hospital. Could you arrange for us to get them?"

The man smiled. "I'll see what I can do."

Within a very short time word arrived at the hospital that the confiscated boxes were being released. Could someone come for them?

Could someone come! Florence and Ervin thanked the Lord for this miracle—for it truly was a miracle. And the biggest miracle was that the supplies were released free of all customs charges!

At that time, a number of young Americans lived in Vietnam, sent by their government to help the new country learn to be independent. The group was called the United States Operation Mission (USOM). Some of the wives came to the hospital for their prenatal care. Every few days one of them would ask, "Doctor, when will the hospital inpatient department be ready?"

The reply was always the same. "We don't have the funds to complete the remodeling. Besides it takes a lot of money for operating-room equipment and to furnish all the rooms."

One of these women, Mrs. Mann, was the wife of the USOM medical adviser. Mrs. Mann talked to her husband, begging him to help the hospital.

"Darling, you know I would love to do it," he replied, "but the medical equipment coming from America is destined for use in hospitals all over Vietnam. Besides, it can't be used for a church-sponsored institution."

"But please talk to the Vietnamese minister of health," Mrs. Mann pled with her husband. "See if he won't be willing to help in some way. We wives don't want to go clear to Manila in order to have our babies delivered by American-trained doctors."

The minister of health was not interested in the matter at all.

But Mrs. Mann kept after her husband, saying, "If you don't go and try to persuade him, then I will."

During a brief visit to Singapore, the Wintons noticed an autoclave sitting on a junk pile in back of Youngberg Memorial Hospital. Ervin asked the medical director, Dr. Galen Coffin, if the hospital were actually throwing it away.

"Well, we don't need it anymore," Dr. Coffin replied. "We have a nice new one, so, yes, we are throwing the old one away."

"Give it to the Saigon Adventist Hospital, then," Florence begged. And the Wintons went home with an autoclave.

Installing it was a problem, however. The building did not have enough electrical current available to operate the autoclave; the building needed to be rewired. In addition, no one in Saigon knew how to install an autoclave. So once again Doctor Ervin's nonsurgical skills were called into play. After seeing patients all day, he spent many evenings rewiring the building and hooking up the machine. Florence had already filled it full of surgical and delivery bundles. She was eager to have them all sterilized in case of an emergency.

One company in town donated an air conditioner for the operating room, and it was quickly installed. Workmen covered the walls with white tile. At last the operating room was ready—except there was no furniture for it. Absolutely none.

Florence had been raised in the mission field, however. She wasn't about to let a lack of furniture stop her. She began poking around. In one of the sheds in back of the maternity clinic in Cholon, Florence found an old discarded delivery table with a rusty cast-iron frame.

Hmm, she thought, *this has some possibilities.*

She had the delivery table transported to the Saigon hospital and hired a man to sandpaper the rust from the frame. Then she painted it with a coat of white enamel paint—the first of several that would be needed. She also ordered foam rubber cushions to be made at a local rubber factory.

The morning that her husband hooked up the autoclave, Florence put the last coat of paint on the delivery table. The rubber company assured her the pads would be ready the next day. That evening she and her husband planned to get everything sterilized. But something went wrong with the autoclave solenoid, and the pressure could not be controlled. Finally the doctor rewired it so that he could control it manually. He and Florence stayed up until after midnight sterilizing the first bundles.

Early the next morning Ervin rushed into Florence's office and said, "Florence, get ready quickly! One of the American women is in labor!"

For a second or two, Florence panicked. The paint on the delivery table was still wet; paint doesn't dry rapidly in the tropics. And the pads hadn't arrived. There was no instrument table or any other furniture on the medical floor yet. She rushed over to the Mission office.

"Pastor Wallace," she called out even before she saw him. "I need a big favor! May I borrow that small stand you use for Communion? It's kind of an emergency."

She managed to get it back to the hospital, and one of the helpers carried it up to the operating room for her. The unpadded delivery table was wheeled in, wet paint and all. What else could she do?

Suddenly she remembered two boxes that had come from the Seventh-day Adventist church in Blythe, California. The boxes contained some lovely quilts. Florence hadn't appreciated them when they had first arrived. "What on earth will we do with quilts in the tropics?" she had muttered to herself. But now, she located them and quickly folded several together, wrapping them in a large plastic sheet. Now she had pads on the delivery table.

The sterile bundle was opened up on the small Communion table, and soon she and the doctor were properly attired, each in a new gown, cap, and mask. A few hours later, little John Donnel, Jr. was born—the first baby to be delivered at the Saigon Adventist Hospital.

After delivery, the new mother was moved to the single bed on the unit—one the doctor had brought from his own home. Florence made a bed for the baby in her own laundry basket. The next day the mother and baby were transferred to the guest room in the Wintons' home.

During all this time, Florence had been trying to get some graduate nurses from Bangkok to come to Saigon and help her when the hospital opened fully. But so far no one had responded to her plea. Finally, she appealed to the Manila Sanitarium and Hospital in the Philippines. The nursing supervisor talked with some of the nurses, and four of them volunteered to go to Saigon. They would be the first missionaries ever sent from the Philippines. But Florence knew they couldn't come quite yet—there was no place for them to live. And the hospital wasn't equipped adequately to admit inpatients. Another roadblock also loomed large—with hardly any income, how would the hospital pay the nurses?

Then one day, God gave Florence an idea. She sent an SOS to her mother. Mary Nagel was living in Loma Linda, California, and working as a nurse's aide at Loma Linda Sanitarium and Hospital. Florence begged her mother to come. At first, Mary said No, but Florence wired her again, telling her of the great need for help and urging her to come. Finally Mary said she would come if she could get a passport and a visa for Vietnam. The next day Florence prayed earnestly—and sent her mother the ticket.

Mary Nagel arrived in Saigon the day after baby John was born. And she immediately took over the care of both mother and baby. What a blessing she was to Florence!

The due date for Mrs. Mann grew closer. She still pushed her husband to do something about getting help for the Saigon Adventist Hospital. Finally a plan took shape. The Vietnamese government would loan some of the medical equipment that had been sent to it from America so that the Saigon Adventist Hospital could care for the pregnant mothers of USOM. The permit to pick up the equipment was issued.

It was an answer-to-prayer day for Ervin and Florence when they hired a very large moving van and set out for the warehouse with a driver and an interpreter. The warehouse was on a large island with many other warehouses and a few small villages. It was connected to the city by a narrow bridge. When the great warehouse doors were pushed open, how excited Florence was to see rows of hospital beds, shiny stainless steel basins, and an entire field laboratory setup, including a microscope, centrifuge, colorimeter, glass beakers, and pipettes. And this was only a small section of the warehouse!

The truck was loaded and the doors were closed when suddenly gunshots rang out. Bullets whizzed all around them. Explosions erupted close by. Everyone tried to find shelter behind a nearby brick wall. Fires broke out in a thatched-roof building not far from the warehouse.

An hour later, the gunfire stopped as suddenly as it had begun. A policeman stepped up to Ervin and said, "If you wish to get out of here, I believe now might be a good time!"

CHAPTER SIXTEEN

The Perfect Piece of Property

Florence, Ervin, and their interpreter climbed into the truck's cab with the driver, and they set off down the narrow road and across the bridge. When they entered the main street into Saigon, not a person was in sight. An eerie silence hung over the city. As they turned a corner, they could see in the distance soldiers unloading large guns and ammunition. They also saw troops taking up positions behind buildings and trees.

Florence prayed fervently as they neared the guards. The soldiers commanded them to halt. The interpreter explained who they were and what they had in the truck.

"Hurry!" an officer told them. "Get to the hospital as quickly as possible. The battle will continue very soon."

The truck had barely reached the hospital when they could hear the noise of fighting resume. For the next ten days, the battles continued. When it was all over, Ervin and Florence went to see what had happened. All the warehouses on the island had been burned to the ground! Most of the smaller buildings were also destroyed. Whole blocks of downtown were now nothing but rubble. Roads were still blocked by overturned cars and trucks, most of which had been burned. People were searching through the debris for family members and their personal belongings. The injured, dead, and dying filled the city's hospitals beyond their capacity. And the homeless erected shanties on the sidewalks to shelter themselves.

Later the Wintons learned the cause of the fighting. When President Diem took office, several factions opposed him. One of these was the Ben Sui Yin group that had been hiding on the island where they had gone to get supplies. President Diem had chosen the day the missionaries went to pick up hospital equipment as the day to conquer his enemies. But no one could explain the one-hour lull right after the fighting began. Florence knew the answer, however. Once again, God had shown His care for His work and His workers.

Soon after this experience, a hospital in America contributed its old operating-room lights and several spotlights to the Saigon Adventist Hospital. Another American hospital donated a large X-ray machine. One doctor sent a desperately needed operating-room table. And still another doctor sent anesthesia equipment. Piece by piece, equipment came until the little hospital could hold no more.

In spite of the interest in the new hospital, it didn't generate enough income during its first three months of operation even to pay the salaries of the employees. A Seventh-day Adventist Chinese merchant loaned Florence the payroll money. But from the fourth month on, the hospital was entirely self-supporting. This was largely due to services it offered in prenatal care and baby delivery. A few beds had been put in the upstairs rooms for the American maternity patients, and the maternity hospital in Cholon loaned a Chinese nurse's aide to care for the mothers and babies at night. Florence's mother took care of them in the daytime. The Wintons' cook prepared the meals needed at the hospital. The number of maternity patients increased rapidly. In fact, the Saigon Adventist Hospital earned a new nickname—the baby institution.

In addition to those needing maternity care, a number of patients in the clinic needed surgical help. The time had come for the hospital to open its doors for a full range of surgical and medical services. Florence sent word to the Philippines for the nurses to come at once. She was anxious to have all the nursing care at Saigon Adventist Hospital be provided by Seventh-day Adventist Christians. She didn't want to just compete with the other hospitals in town, she wanted nurses who would pray with their patients and lead them to the Great Physician.

In January 1956, when the Union met in Singapore, Elder Nerness gave a report that summarized the activities of the first seven months the hospital was in operation.

> The Saigon Adventist Hospital was opened May 22, 1955, as a venture of faith with 133,000 piasters (US$3,800.00). It was a happy day when we carried the stored equipment and supplies to the reconstructed building.
>
> The story is thrilling. The institution started in a building that was once a prince's residence until it was bombed out. The property was purchased with the 1948 Thirteenth Sabbath overflow offering. It was remodeled with funds raised in an Ingathering campaign which met with phenomenal success. It was furnished with equipment given in part by the U.S. government within a matter of hours before its warehouse was destroyed, and in part by friends in the city and by physicians in the U.S., Mexico, and the Far East who donated their surplus until today the hospital stands fully equipped and serving with capital assets of more than 1,000,000 piasters (US$50,000.00) in less than a year of operation! Thus another light of cheer has been lit in a dark place.

What a day of rejoicing it was when the nurses arrived from the Philippines! Four of them came: Mr. and Mrs. Gem Rojo, Miss Luz Santa Domingo, and Miss Esther Causing. Mr. Rojo was not only a good nurse but also a trained anesthetist, laboratory technician, and radiology technician. Mrs. Rojo became the superintendent of nurses. The first thing she did was organize a class to train nurse's aides.

The staff was growing so fast, it was hard to keep up with the expansion. New buildings were purchased for dormitories, and homes were made available for married couples. A complete new wing was added to the front of the original hospital building, providing space for another doctor's office, a nursery, and more patient rooms on the second floor as well as considerably increasing the size of the waiting room on the first floor. The outside of the structure was modernized, and a neon sign was added that could be seen from blocks away. More and more patients came. Almost before the improvements were completed, the hospital needed even more space.

During the Wintons' second year in Saigon, personnel changes at the Vietnam Mission and the Far Eastern Division offices affected the hospital. Pastor Elton Wallace, Mission president, was called to Philippine Union College. Pastor Lester Storz became the president of the Vietnam Mission. And H. Carl Currie became chairman of the hospital board.

Soon after his appointment, Pastor Currie called a meeting of the board. One of the first items on the agenda was a proposal to look for property for a new, expanded hospital facility. The vote was unanimous in favor of doing so.

After some searching, a seven-acre lot was found that would be perfect for the hospital's needs. The property boasted a large, fully furnished French villa with three floors of living space, plus servants' quarters and a four-car garage in the rear. There was also easy access to the main boulevard leading from the airport to the palace in the center of town. Pastor Storz learned that the villa belonged to a French organization, and that two of the partners had already returned to Paris. The third partner, Mr. Paulan, remained in town to dispose of the property.

Florence and Pastor Storz visited Mr. Paulan to inquire about the land. The price was 1,400,000 piasters—about US$40,000. All the profits of the current hospital operation were being poured back into the improvements and expansion that had been taking place at that facility. Therefore, the asking price for this property was about US$40,000 more than the hospital had in disposable income! It seemed outrageous even to talk to Mr. Paulan about buying the property, but Florence wanted that piece of land. She felt God wanted it too. And if God wanted it, He would bring in the money somehow. Florence and Pastor Storz told Mr. Paulan that they must talk the matter over with the members of the hospital board, but that they would give him a reply in one week.

They sent letters to Pastor Currie and the other members of the board. During that week, Pastor Walter Beach, from the General Conference, was touring Asia and had a short layover in Saigon. Pastor Storz quickly made arrangements to allow him to leave the airport so that he could see the new property that was being considered. Pastor Beach felt that God's hand was indeed clearly leading in finding this perfect piece of land. In reality, it was the only piece of land that size for sale in the Saigon city limits. The other available lots were too far out of town to be convenient for patients.

By the end of the week, no reply had come from the board chairman, Pastor Currie. At morning worship, Mission personnel offered special prayers asking God to lead in the matter. The local board members all felt that the land should be purchased. So Pastor Storz and Florence went to see Mr. Paulan again. His face lit up when he met them, and his handshake was warm and friendly. His partners had sent word for him to make a deal with the Adventist hospital. They would not even require a down payment! Florence turned to Pastor Storz, her face beaming with joy.

He smiled and needlessly asked, "Shall we buy it?"

"Certainly." Her reply came without a second of hesitation.

The terms were drawn up, giving the hospital one year to pay for the property, with no interest charge, no down payment, and immediate occupancy. The first payment was due when the property cleared escrow, the balance to be paid in two equal payments. And Mr. Paulan handed Florence the key to the villa.

Florence and Pastor Storz walked out of the office, their hearts overflowing with rejoicing. Florence knew God's hand had prepared the way. When they reached the hospital, they shared the good news, and excitement spread rapidly through the entire staff. The workers thrilled at the thought of a new hospital in the near future—one with room to turn around without bumping into anything or anyone.

During the following week, the gateman at the new property informed Pastor Storz that Mr. Paulan had brought some Americans to look over the villa and grounds. The pastor immediately set out to find Mr. Paulan.

"I don't understand, sir," he said when he faced Mr. Paulan in his office. "We signed a contract in good faith. How is it that you are showing the property to someone else?"

"Please do not worry," Mr. Paulan replied in a soothing tone. "Some Americans from the Standard Oil Company are interested in purchasing the property. I told them it was already sold. But they begged to see it, so I took them out and showed them around. Then they wanted to know what I had sold it for. They offered me double the price. But I told them that the land was sold and that the deal could not be changed no matter what they offered me."

When Pastor Storz reported the conversation to Florence, she felt relieved—and thankful. Surely the Lord must have worked on Mr. Paulan's heart to make him stick to his contract even though not a cent had yet been paid! He was indeed a man of his word.

About a month later the gateman came to Pastor Storz and Florence once again. This time he tracked them down in church on Sabbath morning. He was so excited—or upset—that he could hardly speak. When he finally blurted out his message, Florence felt a cold shiver run down her back.

"Sir," the gateman began. "A contractor brought his whole crew to the property this morning. And they are still there, laying out the property for a large housing project!"

Pastor Storz left church immediately and accompanied the gateman back to the villa. The men were hard at work, just as the gateman had said. Pastor Storz found the contractor and confronted him.

"You cannot do this," he said. "This property has been purchased by the Saigon Adventist Hospital. Please take your men away immediately."

The contractor gave a smug grin. "Look at this," he said, holding up an official-looking document. "This land has been requisitioned by the government for the construction of refugee housing!"

CHAPTER SEVENTEEN

Beginning With an Impossibility

Pastor Storz stared at the contractor and then at the paper he held up.

"There has obviously been a mistake," Pastor Storz told him. "Would you please cease construction until I can look into this matter?"

The contractor considered this a moment before he replied. "Yes, I will take my men away until we have further orders."

Again, Pastor Storz hunted up Mr. Paulan, who expressed surprise to hear that the government had sent a contractor to the property.

"Yes," he said, "the government requisitioned the land more than four months ago, but the law is clear about these requisitions. It specifically states that if building has not begun within three months of the time the order was issued, the owner is free to sell his property. So I legally sold it to you."

Together the men set out to talk to the government authorities. When they arrived at the proper office, they were informed that the minister had gone to Australia for several weeks to attend the Olympics. His assistant said he could not change the order requisitioning the land, but he would issue a command to stop construction until the minister returned and produced the original order. Again God intervened, and the new hospital property was still theirs—at least until the minister returned. When he came back and heard that the property had been sold for a new hospital, he was delighted. He voided the original requisition immediately.

Contributions from local friends and businesses funded the first two payments to Mr. Paulan. When Florence's family and some American doctors heard about the land purchase, they also wanted a share in helping to pay for the new hospital property. Soon the Mission was able to make the third payment—and owned the new property free and clear.

But one more obstacle suddenly arose. A new law came into effect that no foreigners could own property in Vietnam. Legally, all of the Mission-owned property was held in the name of Pastor Elton Wallace. In addition, the government considered the Mission a French organization, and French organizations could not buy property—even to build a hospital. Negotiations began between the Vietnamese ambassador and the General Conference of Seventh-day Adventists in Washington, D.C.

One year and six months later, on America's Thanksgiving Day in 1956, President Diem signed the papers that allowed the property to belong to the Seventh-day Adventist Church. What a day of thanksgiving that was! Now the property only waited for the new hospital to be erected.

The financial picture at the Saigon Adventist Hospital was looking up. All the money borrowed to get it started had been repaid. For the first time since the hospital had been only a chalk drawing on the floors of a vacant building, its books were in the black. Florence was doubly elated. It had been well worth all the work she had done. God was definitely blessing the hospital.

The Wintons had a little more than a year until furlough time, and Florence had one more problem to deal with. It was a big problem. Beginning with the war for Vietnam's independence, refugees had built small shelters on every available spot of empty land—including the new hospital property. Over the years, these squatters had made themselves very much at home. Some had actually built small houses and planted gardens. Before the hospital could be built, these squatters would have to be moved off the property. But as in some other Asian countries, the squatters would not move unless they were paid—and paid well. Only then could the Mission build a brick wall around the property.

This problem, too, was resolved. The squatters were paid, and the wall was built—all before the Wintons left on furlough. Florence happily wrote the check to pay for the iron gate at the entrance. She greatly anticipated seeing the new hospital under construction when the family returned in a year. Of course, it would take several years to complete the hospital facility, and the money for construction must be earned before the board would allow them to proceed.

In the meantime, the villa was remodeled into three apartments for families and several studio apartments for unmarried graduate nurses. A church school for the American children met in a room on the third floor. It was a happy moment for Florence when she and her family spent their first night sleeping on the new property.

This second year at the hospital had been a busy one, as the year-end reports recorded. Medical personnel saw 40,000 outpatients and admitted 758 patients to the hospital. They delivered 103

The original Saigon Adventist hospital as it appeared in 1960 after it had been remodeled several times.

babies and performed 147 major surgeries. The staff had grown to more than fifty employees, and every staff member was a baptized church member—an especially important statistic for Florence.

With all the nursing help now in place, Florence's mother, Mary Nagel, was finally free to return home. Mary suggested that she take her grandchildren with her to the United States. Things were so hectic right then for Florence, she pointed out. There was a hospital to run, one to build, and frequent armed conflicts around the area. Billy was six years old, and his sister was only a year younger. The separation would be hard, but Florence and Ervin felt the children would be safer in America with their grandma. And their furlough began in six months, so it wouldn't be a long separation.

During these years, the gospel was spreading rapidly in Vietnam. The Vietnamese *Voice of Prophecy* had gone on the air as a result of Dr. Winton's care of a grateful patient. Then the brother of Paul Hung, husband of Lillian, Florence's friend from China days, came to Saigon to help prepare programs for the *Voice of America*. Paul explained to his brother how wonderful it would be if the *Voice of Prophecy* could be given in Chinese over the air. This hadn't been done even in Taiwan yet. If it could be arranged, people all over Southeast Asia could hear the weekly program in Chinese. But they had no Chinese quartet—and who would be the speaker?

Finally his brother said, "Paul, you write the script. Then come in, and I will record it in my studio and play it over my station."

When Paul shared his excitement with Florence, she said, "This is wonderful! I just learned that the King's Heralds quartet is recording a number of songs in Chinese. Pastor Milton Lee has just been to America and has arranged this with the King's Heralds."

Pastor Lee let Paul make a copy of these recordings. When the first Chinese *Voice of Prophecy* program went on the air, it was given in two Chinese dialects. But it was the music that initially captured the listening audience. People called the station asking about the singers and the beautiful organ music. "Where were such singers and organists to be found in Saigon?" they wanted to know. When they were told that the music came from Americans, they were amazed.

Even though Paul and Lillian Hung worked full time—and even overtime—at the hospital, they still found time to develop these programs. Whenever they had an afternoon off, they went to the radio station to make recordings. As Christmas neared that year, the station manager requested that Paul arrange special Christmas programs—one for each day of the week before Christmas. Many of the hospital workers helped by singing solos or duets and by giving special readings. The choirs of the two Saigon Adventist churches got together to record some wonderful music, including selections from Handel's *Messiah*.

About this time, church members asked Florence and Ervin to visit George Ngo, a man who had once been an Adventist Christian, but who had lost his way. He had completed the nurse's course at Eden Hospital in Fat Shan, China, but during the war years he had fled to Saigon, where he married a girl who had no use for the Christian faith. George soon quit attending church as well. Now he had contracted tuberculosis and was in a sanitarium for treatment.

When the Wintons visited him, they found a very sick man. George lay on the bed, coughing weakly. His condition deteriorated rapidly over the next few weeks. One morning after a severe hemorrhage, George turned his face towards the wall and prayed—his first prayer in a long, long time.

"Dear God," he prayed, "if You will heal me, I will serve You the rest of my life."

In a very short time, George left the hospital on his own two feet, a well man. And he didn't forget his prayer. After his rebaptism, he joined the Saigon Adventist Hospital staff, where his skills were greatly needed. His angry wife took their little son and moved out of their home. George was crushed, but he didn't give up his newly regained faith. He prayed earnestly that God would soften his wife's heart and bring her and their son back to him.

It was at this time that the hospital workers were preparing the Christmas radio programs. George came to Florence with a suggestion. "My wife has a beautiful soprano voice," he said. "If you invited her, she might be willing to come and sing with us."

George's wife did join the singing group. She made friends with some of the hospital staff and other church members who were helping out in the programs. Soon she was bringing her son to Sabbath School and staying for church. George was beside himself with delight. After several months, his family was reunited, and his wife was baptized. George worked in the hospital for many years. Then he accompanied a patient to America and found work at the White Memorial Hospital in Los Angeles, where his wife soon joined him. Their son took the pre-dental course at La Sierra College and went on to become a dentist.

Another example of the hospital's evangelistic outreach occurred when an English-speaking Vietnamese lady was admitted to the hospital as a maternity patient. Dr. Winton asked her where she had learned her beautiful English, and she told him she had attended a university in the United States. There she had met a young Vietnamese man, and they were married. Now they had been invited to return to Vietnam to help with the English programming on Radio Saigon.

That morning a recording by Elder H. M. S. Richards, the founder of the *Voice of Prophecy,* was played on the hospital public-address system. And, of course, the King's Heralds were part of the program.

As the doctor made his usual morning rounds, the lady asked, "Doctor, what is that beautiful program that is being broadcast this morning?"

"It's called the *Voice of Prophecy,*" he replied.

"Well, I'm enjoying it very much. You know, my husband is looking for this type of program for his new English radio station. I think he would be very interested in getting in touch with this program. Could you help him?"

Of course, the doctor could help him! He gave her some tapes for her husband to audition. Later he also gave her husband the address where he could arrange to get the *Voice of Prophecy* programs regularly. Her husband was so pleased with the program that he scheduled it on Radio Saigon every Sunday morning at eight o'clock.

That first Sunday, the missionaries gathered around the radio to hear the first broadcast. But when eight o'clock came and the previous program ended, there was nothing but silence on the radio for several minutes. Then the announcer spoke, "And now you will hear the latest news of the day."

What had happened? Another period of silence. And then a familiar sound came over the air. A male quartet sang, "Lift up the trumpet and loud let it ring. Jesus is coming again!" Elder H. M. S. Richards and the King's Heralds were on the air in English over Radio Saigon. What a thrilling moment that was!

Later the missionaries learned what had happened to cause the awkward introduction to that first program. Someone had forgotten to erase the old introduction to the news program. But the missionaries thought it was prophetic—the latest news of the day was indeed the news that Jesus is coming again. That was why Saigon Adventist Hospital had been founded.

And then it was furlough time. The years in Vietnam had gone by quickly. Just a few weeks before the Wintons were to leave on furlough, Pastor Currie wrote that Dr. Edwin Brooks and his wife, Letha, would be transferred from the Adventist hospital in Taiwan to the Saigon Adventist Hospital. Letha and her first husband, Dr. Elmer Coulston, had been missionaries in China when Florence was a girl. She remembered hearing of Dr. Coulston's tragic death. And now, Letha was back in the mission field with her second husband, Edwin Brooks. How Florence admired her!

Letha was a graduate nurse and could help organize the nursing school Florence had dreamed of. There was a dire need for locally trained nurses. Florence and Esther Rojo had already organized a class of girls who had been studying and working at the hospital. Now that the students had a knowledge of English and a good practical hospital background, Letha could carry on.

For a solid week before the Wintons left for their furlough, their friends and former patients gave them one farewell after another. They even had two banquets on the same day. One was at the home of a wealthy Chinese patient. Lillian had told the family that the doctor and his wife didn't eat meat. So the hosts lovingly planned a special meal. Unfortunately, they didn't consider fish or fowl to be "meat." Each of the fourteen courses consisted of one or the other! The soup was made of chicken feet, claws and all floating in the broth! Another course featured fried sparrows—with the heads still intact! Florence had the most trouble with the platter on which lay a whole fish with its eye staring at her. Of course the hostess politely served this head to Florence as the lady guest of honor! Florence was relieved when the last course was finished. She may not have enjoyed the food, but she couldn't help but be touched by the sincere appreciation these people felt for the healing they had received in the hospital.

The Cholon church gave the Wintons a large banquet at one of the restaurants in town. It seemed as if each group tried to outdo the previous one.

Then came the last night—when the hospital staff said Goodbye. Florence's tears flowed freely. These people were her family. Many had come from small villages with a meager education. And now they were doing a marvelous task in caring for the sick in the hospital. The nurses from the Philippines had proved most efficient indeed and were worthy of the honor of being the first Adventist missionaries sent out from that country.

The final act of that last evening was a dress parade. The staff had lovely Vietnamese costumes tailored for both Ervin and Florence. Someone placed a lei of orchids around Florence's neck. A medal carved from ivory was presented to Ervin. On it were carved the words, "First Medical Missionary to Vietnam." The staff had one last request of Florence and Ervin—whenever the Wintons told the story of the Saigon Adventist Hospital, they must wear these costumes.

At three o'clock on the morning of April 28, 1958, Florence made out the checks for the hospital payroll. A few hours later she turned over the accounting books to Dr. Brooks. Weary and exhausted, she sobbed at the airport as she and her husband said Goodbye to the crowd gathered there. She was going back home, but her heart would stay behind in Vietnam.

CHAPTER EIGHTEEN

Alaska or Bust

As the plane left the runway, Florence wiped her tears and tried to focus on the wonderful days ahead. She and Ervin were taking a trip around the world—just the two of them. Over the last few years, they had become so busy that they didn't spend time together, talking and sharing with each other, as they once had. This trip around the world would give them a chance to revitalize their marriage.

In Bangkok, they visited friends; in Burma, they toured ancient ruins. From New Delhi, they journeyed to view the much-talked-about Taj Mahal. The beautiful building was an absolutely breathtaking sight. What an incredible demonstration of a man's love for his wife! Its beauty reminded Florence of the homes God is preparing in heaven for His faithful children. But it was hard to imagine even the heavenly homes being lovelier than the Taj Mahal.

After a brief stop in Karachi, Pakistan, they went on to Beirut, Lebanon, where they spent two days with Arthur and Olive Fund. Arthur had been the best man at their wedding in Camp Crowder fourteen years earlier, but they hadn't seen him since. The Funds took Florence and Ervin to some ruins dating back to the time of King Ahab. Florence noticed that Ervin smiled and laughed more as he relaxed with his old army buddy.

Next they visited the Holy Land. A thrill ran through Florence as she stood on the Mount of Olives, the place from which Jesus had left this earth two thousand years earlier. In Bethlehem Florence tried to imagine angels singing in the sky over a field to announce Jesus' birth. But the sounds of gunfire in the distance made it difficult to concentrate on such details in this town where Jesus had been born.

Florence and Ervin spent a month in northern Africa, seeking out the places where Joseph and Moses had lived. Together they poked through the wares in the local bazaars and sampled the food. Ervin seemed interested in all the sights and sounds, but Florence wondered what he was thinking. He was so silent most of the time.

On the way to Nairobi, Kenya, they flew over Mount Kilimanjaro, the highest peak in Africa. For two weeks Florence's uncle and aunt, Pastor and Mrs. Ernest Hanson, showed them around Kenya. The Hansons had been missionaries in Africa for more than forty years.

The Wintons even joined a safari into one of the big game parks. Florence was excited to see wild animals in their own habitats—and to see them everywhere she looked. One night as they stood outside their hut, Florence slipped her hand into Ervin's. Together they listened to the roar of lions in the distance, and a shiver ran through her. Ervin put his arm around her; she leaned her head against him. It was a special moment for Florence, deep in the heart of Kenya.

They would have loved to stay longer in Kenya, but Florence was also eager to see her brother. Dr. Sherman Nagel, Jr. and his wife, Edith, had lived in Nigeria for the last twenty years. Florence and Sherman had seen little of each other since medical school.

The area around the mission hospital at Ile-Ife, Nigeria, reminded Florence of the scenery in Thailand. For two interesting weeks Florence and Ervin helped Sherman in the hospital so that he could take time off to show them some of the sights of Nigeria.

When this wonderful visit was over, Florence and Ervin flew to Rome. Seeing places where the apostle Paul visited and walking through the Vatican brought history and prophecy to life. In Switzerland, they visited reminders of the Reformation. In Brussels, Belgium, they took in the 1958 World's Fair, which was in full swing. Then it was on to Amsterdam, The Hague, and London.

By the time they arrived in New York, Florence could hardly absorb any more sights or sounds. She and Ervin were eager to get home to their children, and soon they were in a plane again, on the way to California.

And there at last stood Billy and Bunny—their little faces smashed against the fence, watching the plane land. As soon as the door of the plane opened, the guard allowed the children to run out to meet their mother and daddy. The nine months of separation seemed a lifetime to Florence as she hugged Billy and Bunny. As the four Wintons held hands and walked toward the gate, Florence finally saw her own mother and father and many other relatives waiting to greet them. It was a glorious homecoming!

But the Wintons had only two days to visit with all these relatives because the General Conference session was about to begin in Cleveland, Ohio. Florence and Ervin were delegates to the session, representing Vietnam. So taking Billy and Bunny with them, they hurried back across the United States to Ohio. All four marched in the mission pageant, dressed in the native Vietnamese clothes given to them at their farewell party.

The rest of their furlough sped by as rapidly as it began. It seemed to them that it had hardly begun before the time was drawing near for them to return to Vietnam. But before they could do so, they all had to have physical examinations. During Ervin's exam, the doctor found that the strain of the last five years was affecting his health. The doctor advised him not to return to the Mission hospital at that time. He needed a change of pace.

Florence and Ervin decided he should take a year's residency in anesthesiology. They sent a telegram to the Far Eastern Division asking for a leave of absence to take this new training. It was soon settled. Florence also looked forward to a year of rest—and a year focusing on her children and her husband.

Before Ervin finished his studies, an opening came for him to take over a medical practice in Ketchikan, Alaska. The children jumped up and down at the thought of it. Alaska! Way, way up north! They had heard about Alaska because that great frontier had officially gained statehood on January 3, 1959, just a few months earlier. After much reflection and prayer, Ervin and Florence decided to accept this opportunity.

While Ervin finished his residency requirements, Florence threw herself into packing and preparation. In the midst of all her tasks, she couldn't help mourning for her beloved Orient. She didn't understand why God didn't send them back to Vietnam, but God knew best. He had always guided her, and she had always found joy in working for Him. "Thy will be done, Lord," she prayed.

Most of their household belongings were finally packed and shipped. In the back of their Pontiac station wagon, they made a bed for Billy and Bunny to rest on during the long drive from California to Prince Rupert, British Columbia. Their bicycles were tied on top, along with the suitcases. The little Hillman (the car Ervin would use for house calls) was fastened to the rear of the station wagon by a metal A-frame. With Daddy's help, Billy and Bunny painted "Alaska or Bust" on the side windows and across the back of the Hillman. When they started the drive north, people smiled at them and honked their horns and waved. The Wintons were quite a sight!

For three days they drove north, finally arriving at the Canadian border on a Friday. They crossed into British Columbia and spent Sabbath with former classmates in Vancouver. Then they hurried on. They had to reach Prince Rupert before the end of September when the last car ferry to Alaska left port. After September, the next ferry going north wouldn't sail until May. The drive up the Fraser River Gorge was breathtaking. But when they drove from Prince George to Prince Rupert, the scenery became so striking that Florence declared she had never seen anything that could compare with it anywhere in all her travels around the world. The snow-capped peaks sparkled with blue and green glaciers reflecting in the lakes beside the newly built freeway. The valleys were covered with wildflowers in every shade of the rainbow.

The children kept begging their daddy to stop whenever they saw large patches of blueberries, thimble berries, or red currants. He did stop briefly now and then. How good the fruit tasted! And while they sampled the berries, Billy's new Chihuahua puppy, Ginger, romped in the meadow. Billy kept close track of Ginger, knowing other animals might not like a puppy running around their meadow—animals such as the moose, wolves, and bears they saw on the trip.

To reach Prince Rupert, they had to follow a detour so deep in mud that the Pontiac couldn't tow the Hillman through it. They had to disconnect the Hillman and drive it separately. The beautiful sunshine had turned into a downpour. By the time they reached Prince Rupert that evening, no one could tell that the original colors of the station wagon were a rather attractive red and white!

The family had slept in the two cars every night on the trip up the West Coast, so when they crawled into actual motel beds that night in Prince Rupert, it felt like they were sleeping on clouds. The next morning dawned almost dry; only a light drizzle reminded them of yesterday's storm. The children begged to go outside and look around.

Soon they came running back into the motel yelling, "Daddy! Daddy, come see! A tire on the Hillman is busted!" Sure enough, a tire was flat. Ervin had to hurry to get it repaired because cars going on the ferry had to be at the dock before ten o'clock in the morning. Somehow, all was ready when the *Prince George* steamed up to the dock. Its red and white smokestacks looked tall and beautiful.

As the ferry started up the Inland Passage, Florence saw small fishing villages on the islands they passed. Totem poles stood in many of these villages. At last, the *Prince George* steamed around an island, and the passengers could see in the distance the smoke from the sawmills of Ketchikan. As they neared, Florence saw that the city reached from the water's edge up the sides of the mountains. There wasn't much flat land in Ketchikan.

The Winton family—Florence, Ervin, Billy, and Bunny—in Ketchikan, Alaska.

Adventist church members gave them a friendly welcome, and it didn't take long for the Wintons to settle into their new home.

Alaska was a completely new world for them. Forests covered the low mountains, and snow glistened on the higher peaks behind. Instead of a bustling city like Saigon or Bangkok, Ketchikan was a small town. If you wanted to go for a drive, you could travel the whole twenty-six miles of its one paved road in a very short time. The Adventist church, built by the members themselves, boasted a membership of about one hundred people. Most of the Adventists, however, lived out on the huge floating log rafts and cut timber for a living. In fact, one raft was inhabited entirely by

Seventh-day Adventists. They had even built a church and a school on the raft.

Florence grew to love the people in Ketchikan. The social life of the church members in the town centered around the church and school. A large gymnasium, built above the classrooms, was used by the students during the long winters and wet summers, as well as by the church members for potlucks and evening get-togethers.

Ketchikan was so famous for its heavy rainfall and gloomy days that Florence decided to check it out for herself. For a whole year she kept track of the weather every day. The results bore out the reputation. On only thirty days out of the three hundred sixty-five did the sun shine for at least one hour! No wonder the children looked pale.

Florence felt depression creeping in. It wasn't that the weather was so cold. Ketchikan was actually warmer than Seattle on most days. But Florence experienced a recurring feeling that something bad was about to happen. She prayed earnestly that God would help her to be happy. And she really was content, she told herself. The Lord had always helped her to be joyful wherever He led her, and she really did love Ketchikan. When the sun actually shone, it was a beautiful place to live. The children enjoyed their new friends and their new school. In the summers they attended a great youth camp at White River. Both Billy and Bunny had been baptized. Her husband seemed to enjoy his new practice.

So what was wrong?

For more than three years Florence struggled with this question. Was it because the closeness that she and Ervin had begun to reestablish on their trip around the world seemed to have vanished? Certainly he was working long hours, frequently remaining at the hospital all night. Often he spent Sabbath mornings at the hospital too. Lately he seemed to be finding all kinds of reasons to stay away from church functions. And from home.

"Please, Lord," she prayed, "help me. What's happening to my marriage? What can I do to make it right?"

She spent many long hours in prayer, but nothing seemed to change. Maybe things would get better if they could go to San

Francisco to the General Conference session coming up soon. Florence hoped that seeing all their old friends and hearing of the progress of the mission work in the Far East would be the encouragement Ervin needed.

Then one day in the summer of 1963 the telephone rang. Florence reached for the phone, pulled her hand back, then reached over and picked it up.

"Hello?" she said.

"Hello, Mrs. Winton. Do you have a minute to talk?" Before he gave his name, she recognized the voice of the lawyer she and Ervin had used in setting up Ervin's practice.

"Yes." Why did his question sound so ominous?

"Mrs. Winton, I'm sorry to ask this, but has Dr. Winton talked to you about getting a divorce?"

CHAPTER NINETEEN

What Next, Lord?

"A div ... div ... divorce?" Florence steadied herself by grabbing the arm of a chair. Then she collapsed into it. "No, he hasn't said a word."

The lawyer cleared his throat before he continued. "Your husband came into my office this morning and filled out the papers. I was afraid he hadn't told you."

Florence's world crumbled around her. Whatever the lawyer said during the rest of the conversation, she heard very little.

"Why, Lord, why?" she cried as she paced the floor for hours. "Have You forsaken me completely? Don't I matter to You anymore? What am I supposed to do now?"

Billy and Bunny were away at youth camp, and she was grateful to be alone. For hours she fought with God and struggled to gain some measure of control over herself. From somewhere in her heart a voice seemed to speak to her. *You still have your children,* it said. *Now, they are your mission field.*

Finally, she bowed her head and humbly prayed, "Yes, Lord, I do still have the children. They will be my mission field."

★ ★ ★ ★ ★

Bad news travels fast, they say. Before long, Pastor and Mrs. Jim Hiner called her. He had been the pastor in Ketchikan when the Wintons had first arrived; now he was a district pastor in Oregon.

"Florence," he said. "I'm sure you have a lot of packing and sorting to do, so how about letting us care for your children until you get moved. We live in Lebanon, Oregon, now. It's beautiful here, and there's a fantastic church school. You might even consider moving to Lebanon."

"It sounds lovely," she replied sadly. "I don't know where God wants me. He doesn't seem to be talking to me right now."

"Hey, that doesn't sound like the Florence I know. You've lost your footing for a short time, but you'll find it again. By the way, I've been asked to be the conference evangelist, and I'll be holding meetings around the state. If you lived here, you could help with the meetings that are close to home. How about it?"

Florence realized his advice was wise. Nothing could help her forget her troubles better than to work for the salvation of others. Perhaps this was the Lord's hand, using a friend to guide her. Before long, she signed the divorce papers and closed the book on her life in Alaska.

God led Florence to find a new home in the beautiful foothills of the Willamette Valley near the small city of Lebanon, Oregon. The house was on an acre of land near the South Fork of the Santiam River, nestled amidst picturesque mountains and lakes. Billy, twelve, and Bunny, eleven, loved their new home. And they threw themselves wholeheartedly into the Lebanon-Sweet Home Pathfinder Club. And because Florence had promised the Lord that her children would be her mission field, she joined it also. Before long she finished the requirements to become a Master Guide. Not long after that, she became leader of the club. Her home became the clubhouse. It was a thrilling challenge for her to find activities for these young people and to see them carry off honors at the yearly Pathfinder fairs and the camporees.

About the time Florence was well launched into Pathfinders, her brother Sherman and his family came home from Africa on furlough. Their son Charles wanted to attend Milo Academy in southern Oregon in the fall. Would Aunt Florence let him spend his summers and holidays with her?

"Me, too, Aunt Florence," said his sister Betty. "I'll be old enough next year to go to Milo. Can I come, too?"

And that is how Florence soon found herself with four young people living with her. What a wonderful time they had together!

Florence loved working in her beautiful yard. And she found she really needed the occupation. Working with the soil helped when her mind began to betray her, reminding her of all the bad things that had happened to her and filling her with discouragement. During this time, digging in the earth and talking to God became the main support of her life—along with helping in an occasional evangelistic series.

About four days before Christmas, Florence and the children began the drive from Oregon to Loma Linda, California, to visit her parents and to spend some time in warmer weather. Driving south, she found the orchards filled with leafless trees, and from their frozen branches hung foot-long icicles. Farther south, in the higher elevations, snow had turned the tall evergreens into a Christmas wonderland. The weather forecast predicted another severe storm blowing down from the north. Fortunately, the old car kept chugging and stayed just ahead of the bad weather.

When Florence arrived at her parents' home, it was with a sense of relief from the strain of the long drive. Now she could relax and not listen to the weather reports. But it was a short-lived respite. Early the next morning, Florence was called to the phone.

"Hello?" she said.

"Oh, Florence!" said the voice of her neighbor back home in Oregon. "I'm so glad we found you. You must come home immediately."

A knot began to form in Florence's stomach. "What happened?"

"Well, a dam broke on the Santiam River . . . and there's been a flood."

"Is it bad?" Florence asked, not really wanting to hear the answer.

"Yes, it's very bad," the neighbor said. "Right now there are nineteen inches of muddy water in your living room. Most of your beautiful fruit trees and bushes are gone. I'm so sorry to bring you such bad news. We're doing our best to save your things, but we really need you to come home."

Florence hung up the phone and stood still for several minutes—white and shaken. How could there have been a flood when only two days before it had been freezing weather? What did the neighbor mean when she said they were trying to save her things?

"Oh, dear Lord, not more troubles." Tears streamed down her face as she prayed. "Help me, please! I don't know how much more I can take."

As she walked into the kitchen where breakfast was being served, Florence felt like a sleepwalker.

"Mother, what's wrong?" Bunny asked, jumping up out of her chair and going to Florence. "What's happened, Mother?"

Florence gave herself a mental shake before she spoke.

"Well, kids, I hope you have enjoyed your visit with your grandparents because we have to go home immediately."

The announcement brought shocked looks and questions—and then action. Grandpa Nagel called the California Highway Patrol office to find out which roads were open. Some roads had been washed away in places; others were covered by mudslides. He also learned that the rivers in northern California were at flood stage. One more hard rain, and they would overflow their banks. He urged his daughter to wait a day or so for things to stabilize, but Florence insisted on leaving immediately. By the time she brought the car to the front door, Billy and Bunny were waiting with repacked suitcases. It was decided that Betty and Charles should remain with their grandparents and return to Oregon after the holidays.

Before Florence, Billy, and Bunny drove away, Grandpa Nagel prayed earnestly for God's protecting hand over them. By the time they reached the landslide area, the road was open. Florence thanked God for His watchcare over their little car. When they reached the mountains that had looked like a wonderland only two days before, they were horrified. Not a flake of snow was left. It was a picture of destruction. Trees, logs, and parts of buildings had cascaded down in the overflowing rivers. Bridges and highways were washed out, but eventually they drove into their yard—and gasped. Nothing prepared them for the sight.

Bales of hay and drums of gasoline were piled where the rose garden had been. The chain-link fence enclosing the property was bent to the ground on two sides; nearly every post was broken off or twisted. The foundation under the front porch had been washed away, and the house itself was tilted just enough that the front door was jammed open. And where were her precious fruit trees?

As soon as the neighbors saw her car, they came over to help her understand what had happened. The church members—the very dear church members—had taken the furniture and carpets from the house and hosed them down. Then someone took them over to the walnut-drying plant to be thoroughly dried. The Wintons' clothes had been distributed among the different church ladies to be washed. The men had brought hoses into the house and tried to wash the walls and floors. Their kindness overwhelmed Florence—and softened the shock of the disaster.

The neighbors told Florence that a number of her fruit trees were strewn across various front yards along the road.

"How did this happen?" Florence asked. "When we left here, it was a beautiful winter scene."

"Is this your first experience with a chinook?" asked a neighbor.

"What's a chinook?" Bunny asked. "It sounds like an Indian."

"Well, that's because it is an Indian name," another neighbor told her. "A chinook is hot wind that blows through and melts everything in its path. This one took only two days to melt all that snow on the mountains."

The dam on the Santiam River couldn't hold the excessive amount of water. It broke apart, letting the logs and debris cascade over its sides with the noise of clapping thunder. All over the valley, gas and electrical services were out. Fortunately a lot of cut wood had floated onto Florence's property, so she was able to keep a fire burning night and day in the fireplace. The walls were drying out—slowly. Florence took two of the dryer mattresses and stood them up near the fire so they could finish drying and provide padding for sleeping on the floor. The stove, refrigerator, washing machine, and dryer were all filled with mud.

The Public Health Department ordered everyone who lived in the area to be inoculated for typhoid. Florence's body reacted badly to the shot, and she had to go to bed for several days. Lying in bed and feeling terrible gave her time to think about her life. This experience was different than any she had had ever met in the mission field. Once again depression looked her in the face. Tears ran unchecked down her face.

"Why, Lord?" she cried. "Why has this happened? I worked so hard to make a nice home for my family. Don't You care? Am I not doing what You want me to?"

Her children hovered around her, trying to cheer her up. But right then, Florence didn't want to be cheered up. She wanted to be left alone to cry, then sleep, then cry some more.

After a few days of this, a letter arrived:

Dear Florence,
My husband and I will be arriving in the United States on furlough next week. We plan to spend a few days with you, if it's convenient. We look forward to seeing you and the children very soon.
Love,
Alma Milne

Convenient! Oh, how Florence had longed to pour her heart out to her friend—and now she was coming! God *did* care! Florence's world started to look less desolate.

When the Milnes discovered the terrible mess the Wintons were in, they changed their plans and stayed on to help her clean up. Pastor Milne painted the entire house, and his wife scrubbed for days. Florence found comfort and a sense of stability while she scrubbed alongside her girlhood mentor. What a comfort the Milnes had always been to her! It seemed that God had not forgotten her after all. He had sent these kind friends to help her just when she was at her wit's end, stuck in despair and hopelessness.

★ ★ ★ ★ ★

The next year in the early spring, Charles was excited about graduating from Milo Academy, and Billy and Bunny were both going to be finishing elementary school in June. There was a lot of discussion among the family about where they would all go to school the next year. When the time came for the academy seniors to visit a prospective college, Charles chose to visit Pacific Union College.

When he returned, he had a suggestion. "Aunt Florence, I like PUC very much. Can't we move down there?"

Florence hadn't considered this before. She loved PUC too. Then another letter arrived from the Milnes saying they had just bought a retirement house in Angwin, California—the village near Pacific Union College. *Is all this the Lord's way of preparing the way for me to move to California?* wondered Florence.

She wrote immediately to the Milnes and asked if there was another house available in Angwin. She knew houses were scarce on the mountain, but she also knew that if the Lord wanted her there, He'd provide a home. She also sent job applications to the business office of the college and to St. Helena Hospital, a few miles down the hill from PUC. This was a Sunday evening. In the next Friday's mail, two letters arrived. The one from the Milnes described a home with four bedrooms on one acre of land that seemed to answer her needs. The Milnes didn't know the asking price, but they'd try to find out.

The second letter came from St. Helena Hospital offering Florence a choice of several positions and stating they would like her to come down as soon as possible for an interview.

That evening Charles and Betty came home from academy for a long weekend. At sundown worship, Florence told the young people about the letters. After a rousing discussion, she laid the letters on the low table in front of the sofa, and they knelt around them, earnestly praying for God to guide them to do the right thing.

After prayer, they talked further about their options. Each one felt that God was leading them south. Then Monday's mail brought a card from the Milnes saying that Pastor Adlai Esteb, the owner of the house they had described, would be at PUC on Tuesday evening. If Florence were interested at all in the place, she needed to come immediately. Very early the next morning, Florence set out for PUC, praying all the way that her old car would hold together.

Just as she drove up the main street of the campus, she passed Pastor Milne's car. He stopped and guided her to their new home. After supper, the Milnes showed Florence the place they had in mind for her to purchase. Florence was extremely pleased with it—even though she could see only the outside. It was a two-story, old-fashioned home with beautiful large oak trees and evergreens.

Quickly they went back to the Milnes' home and telephoned the place where Pastor Esteb was to stay. His host said he had just arrived. Soon Pastor Esteb was on the phone. He remembered Florence from childhood days in China! No, he had not sold the house yet. In fact, he hadn't even talked to his real estate agent yet. When Florence asked about price and down payment, she was excited. Pastor Esteb asked only two thousand dollars down payment—the exact amount she had in the bank. She could take over his mortgage and pay the balance owed to him as she could handle it. Also, he would deduct the broker's fees. She couldn't believe her ears. Surely God's hand was leading in every detail. So without even seeing the inside of the house, Florence agreed to buy it. A time was set to sign the papers the next day.

Later she learned that three other people had also planned to buy the house. She was convinced that God was watching out for her. In fact, it seemed that God was not just opening doors—He was shoving her through them!

Like a homing pigeon, she had returned to the very place she had longed to be when she was a girl. Here she was again, starting a new chapter in her life.

For the next ten years, Angwin was her home. Here the children finished growing up and getting educated. As she looked at each of her children, she clearly saw that one did not need to cross oceans to be a missionary. During the years in Angwin, she often spoke at surrounding churches, telling about the wonderful things God had done for her all through her life. She was content where God had led her. But a tiny corner of her heart kept longing to revisit her hospital family in Vietnam and her childhood friends in China.

Mary and Sherman Nagel, Florence's parents, a few months before Sherman's death July 6, 1968.

Sherman Jr. and Edith were still in Nigeria, but a civil war had broken out. The Red Cross flew out their youngest son, Jim, and for a little while he made his home with Aunt Florence too. Just before Sherman and Edith began their trip home, Mother Mary Nagel phoned Florence saying that Father was very ill. Florence took a week's vacation and went south to Loma Linda. When she returned to Angwin, she brought her parents to PUC to live in an apartment she had rented for them near her own home.

Sherman and Edith planned to stay in Angwin for a while, too, when they returned to the United States. How nice it would be for them all to be in the same town, together at last. But the night after Florence brought her father to Angwin, he had a massive stroke and died. It was July 6, 1968. Sherman Nagel, that wonderful pioneer missionary to China, had gone to sleep to wait for Jesus to come.

Florence took her mother into her home.

Bunny was the first of the four children to leave home. She married and later provided Florence with three darling granddaughters. Niece Betty finished her training as a nurse and also got married. Nephew Charles graduated from PUC, then took the laboratory technician's course. After he was married, he accepted an invitation to work in Castle Memorial Hospital in Hawaii.

Then one day Billy announced that he, too, was going to be married. Florence's last chick was flying the coop.

But what about the rest of my life? Florence asked herself. *Dear Lord, Bill is about to get married, then Sherman will return from the mission field, and Mother could live with them. No one will need me anymore. Will You? You know I'm past sixty, Lord. Can I still be of service to You? Or am I too old to be a missionary?* These thoughts swirled through her mind often these days.

The idea of further service took hold, and she prayed that God would lead her to where she could be of use to Him. She planned and prayed, and then one day she finally did something about it. She sent an application to the General Conference Mission Board, stating that she was ready to go back to Asia if there was a place for her.

Eventually a letter arrived from the president of the South China Island Union, Pastor Ezra Longway.

"I will be coming to PUC next week," he wrote. "I'd like to visit with you while I'm there. If you're still interested, I'd like to talk to you about going back to Hong Kong."

CHAPTER TWENTY

My Heart's Gone Back to China

"Florence, it's good to see you again," Ezra Longway said as he shook hands with her.

She smiled. "Do come in. It's good to see a friend who can talk about Asia," she said. "How I miss it!"

The two of them sat in her sunny living room and talked about missionaries they both knew, about countries they had lived and worked in, and about mission work in general.

"I'm especially interested," Florence said, "in the new hospitals that I understand have just been built in Hong Kong. I was excited to hear about them."

"Dr. Harry Miller and I worked hard to establish the newest one, the one on Stubbs Road. The hardest part was procuring the land. But God always provides a way for us to do His will. It isn't quite finished yet, and it certainly isn't paid for, but God will provide. Actually, that's one of the reasons I'm here in America. I'll be visiting many of the Chinese doctors and merchants who live here now, raising funds to finish the hospital."

"I wish I could go back to work in China, but I realize China doesn't allow missionaries now. Do you think there would be an opening for a laboratory technician in one of the hospitals in Hong Kong?"

"I'm sure there will be a place for your talents and your dedication," he replied. "Let's keep in touch. And I'll let you know as soon as I hear of an opening for you."

Over the next few months, Florence and he talked often by phone and letter. On Sabbath, June 23, 1973, Florence was in Pleasant Hill, California, to visit her friends, Al and Fawn Roth. She often went to church with them, so she felt right at home there. Over the years, she had shared many of her mission experiences with the Sabbath School in Pleasant Hill, and this Sabbath was no exception.

The Thirteenth Sabbath overflow offering that quarter was to go toward finishing Hong Kong Adventist Hospital, located on Stubbs Road. During the Sabbath School mission report, Florence told about the work of the missionaries in China, starting with her father, Sherman Nagel, the first pastor in Hong Kong, and continuing right down to the present time. Then she added, "Many of you have asked me the same question: 'Are you going back again?'

"I always hoped this would be possible." Her eyes sparkled as she spoke. "Missionaries aren't allowed in China anymore, but this morning I can tell you that I have accepted a call to return to Hong Kong in the very near future.

"In closing, I'd like to read a verse from a poem I wrote long ago—on my sixteenth birthday. It's about China, but Hong Kong is only leased from China and is filled with Chinese people, so it will do just fine!

> "I'm going back to China,
> No more from duty wander.
> My heart turns back to China,
> I can stay here no longer.
>
> I miss the old walled city,
> My home and childhood country.
> My heart's gone back to China,
> And I must go!"

During the remainder of the Sabbath School, her mind was in a whirl. It was really true. Her dream was becoming a reality. "Thank You, Lord," she whispered over and over.

The speaker for church that morning was also a veteran missionary from China, Pastor Ezra Longway. Her eyes caught the smile on his face when he walked on the platform, and her heart skipped a beat. Only a few very close friends knew their secret—but that was about to change.

When Pastor Robert Watts introduced the speaker, he said, "Friends, we have an unusual privilege this morning. We have as our guest speaker Pastor Ezra Longway. He is one of the pioneers of our mission work in the Far Eastern Division. He has spent more than fifty-five years in service there. He and his wife first went to Thailand in 1918. Four years later they moved to the great country of China and labored there continuously until the Japanese occupation when all the missionaries had to leave. During the years of World War II, he remained as president of our church in Free China, until the Communist Party took over and our work behind the Bamboo Curtain had to be closed."

Pastor Watts paused for a breath and then continued. "Then Pastor Longway was called to labor in Japan and later answered an invitation to be director of the newly formed China Island Union with headquarters in Taiwan. He is now officially retired as far as the denomination is concerned. But . . ." Pastor Watts's smile spread across his face, "no one can make this man stop working—not when a mission field calls. Even though his good wife is no longer beside him, Pastor Longway is doing fund-raising here in the United States to complete the new hospital we have all been asked to help with this morning. Soon he will be returning to Hong Kong to do fund-raising there. He is determined that this new hospital will be finished and paid for very soon."

He paused again. He looked straight at Florence with a twinkle in his eyes. Then he continued.

"I have a little surprise I want to share with all of you this morning. Pastor Longway is not returning to the mission field alone. He has asked our beloved Florence Winton to go back with him—as his wife!"

Amid the gasps of surprise in the congregation, Pastor Watts turned to Pastor Longway and asked, "Where did you meet Florence the first time?"

The reply came instantly, "In China."

After the service, Pastor Watts found Florence in the midst of well-wishing friends. When he finally got her aside, he said, "I hope it didn't offend you that I announced your engagement. This was such a very special announcement in the midst of all the talk of mission fields."

"How could I be offended!" she laughed. "I thought my life as a missionary was over. Now God has given me a second chance to work for Him—and a second chance at happiness."

Three months later Florence spent another weekend with the Roths. This time she brought some beautiful satin fabric that Alma Milne had sent from Hong Kong. She had chosen the Oriental bride's traditional color of pink. And the Chinese characters for "blessings on your wedding" had been woven into the brocaded satin. Fawn Roth was going to help Florence cut out her wedding dress.

Ezra Longway was on a two-month trip around the eastern and central United States raising funds for the Stubbs Road hospital. But Florence was never far from his thoughts. He wrote often, and here at the Roths' home she received a huge box of red roses from him. Florence felt her cup of joy running over. She read and reread his letters, looking forward to the day they would go to Hong Kong—together.

She hadn't finished arranging the roses when the phone rang. It was Ezra's voice, reaching across the miles to her.

"Sit down before you fall down," he commanded, after a tender greeting.

What a strange order!

"OK, I'm sitting," she said, sliding into a nearby chair.

"I just received a telephone call from the president of the Far Eastern Division telling me that the General Conference Committee has voted for you to go as a foreign mission appointee to Hong Kong for two years. This means that you'll get paid for your work. You'll not be there just as my wife."

When the call was finished, Florence didn't move. Her mind was looking happily into the future. She would be back in the Orient, perhaps someday even back to the land she called home. Though she was almost sixty-three, her dreams were coming true; she wasn't too old to serve her God as a missionary!

"Thank You, Lord," she prayed. "I'm so happy! You are so good to me."

★ ★ ★ ★ ★

On November 11, 1973, in the presence of many fellow missionaries, Chinese friends, and family, Ezra and Florence

Florence and Ezra Longway, married November 11, 1973.

were married. Ezra was seventy-eight, and Florence was sixty-three. They planned to spend a couple of weeks shopping and packing before beginning their trip to Hong Kong. But problems arose almost immediately. The St. Helena Hospital couldn't find anyone to take over Florence's position. Florence felt a heavy responsibility for her job. How could she leave without her duties being covered? When someone was finally found to fill her position, Florence received a letter from Robert Burchard, the administrator of the Hong Kong Adventist Hospital, asking her to plan on taking charge of the clinical laboratory there when she arrived.

Oh, my! Florence had been working in the purchasing office for the last ten years. Medical science had progressed greatly during that time, and many new methods and techniques were being used in the medical technology field. She knew her skills were outdated. If she could just *work* in the lab, she would learn the new skills gradually. But there was no time for that. She was going to be in *charge!* Immediately she wrote to old friends at the White Memorial Hospital's clinical laboratory, asking permission to come for a crash course to refresh her skills. Their reply came quickly.

"By all means come!" they wrote. "We will be glad to help you in any way we can. And it will be so good to see you again."

The day after she terminated her employment with St. Helena Hospital, Ezra and Florence left for Los Angeles. When Florence walked into the lab at the White Memorial Hospital, she felt as if someone had turned back the clock twenty years! So many faces were familiar—they just had a bit of gray added to their hair. Yet in many ways, it was all different. Some of her former students now were department heads, and the entire laboratory was all new.

Florence took one look at all the modern equipment, and her heart sank. Now she knew what Rip van Winkle felt like when he awoke from his long sleep. But everyone was so kind, and each took time to help refresh her memory and to teach her to use the new equipment. By the end of six weeks, her confidence in her abilities had returned, and she was eager to be on her way to Hong Kong.

The last Friday before Ezra and Florence were to leave for Hong Kong, a letter came for them—written in Chinese characters. Florence hadn't used written Chinese for so long, she couldn't read it.

"You'd better decipher this," she said, handing it to Ezra.

He looked it over and asked, "Do you know someone named Wong Giang Lan?"

"Yes! Indeed I do!" Florence exclaimed. "She was one of my closest friends in China. I haven't heard from her for forty-six years! Read it to me. What does it say?"

"It says that another old friend of yours was visiting in America and heard about our marriage and learned that you had just been working at the White Memorial Hospital. When this friend returned to Taiwan she gave that address to Giang Lan who wrote you this letter, hoping it would catch up with you. She lives in Taipei now." He looked up from the letter and smiled. "Probably you'll be able to find her there when we visit on our way to Hong Kong."

"Oh, Ezra, let's go to the Chinese church in Alhambra tomorrow, shall we? Who knows what old friends we'll find there?"

So in the morning they got up early and drove the sixty miles to Alhambra, California.

"Lotus Blossom! Is that really you?"

Florence whirled around. There was Lucy Wun-Chan, another inseparable friend from her teenage years! As they talked, Florence said, "Lucy, you'll never guess who I received a letter from yesterday!"

Lucy wrinkled her nose. "I never could guess things, remember? Who was it?"

"Giang Lan! She lives in Taipei now, so I'm going to get to see her in a few weeks."

"I haven't heard from her in over forty years," Lucy said. "But my husband and I are going home to Singapore very soon, and we'll go by way of Taipei. So when you see her, tell her I'm coming." Lucy sighed. "It's terrible the way we lose track of each other."

February 11, 1974—the last pack-

Mary Nagel and Florence Longway at their final parting on February 11, 1974. Both knew they would probably never see the other again on this earth.

ing was done. Around the breakfast table in Sherman and Edith's home sat Billy and his wife Pam, Mary Nagel, and two old friends of Ezra's, Dr. and Mrs. Paul Quimby. Ezra and Dr. Quimby had been classmates in college, and both had served their church in China for many years. After everyone had finished eating, Sherman read from the Bible, and Dr. Quimby prayed, beseeching God to pour out His rich blessings upon Ezra and Florence as they returned once more to the mission field.

Then came the most difficult moment—saying goodbye to Florence's mother. She and Father had said Goodbye to Sherman and Florence many times over the last twenty-five years. But this time was different. Now Mary Nagel was a widow, and she had passed her eighty-sixth birthday. Florence was certain she would never see her mother again on this earth.

They both choked back the tears as Mother took Florence's hands in hers and said, "I want you to go and hurry and get the task done so that we may all go home with Jesus."

CHAPTER TWENTY-ONE

Lotus Blossom Returns

Florence looked out the window and watched the ground drop away as the plane gained altitude. She reached over and squeezed Ezra's hand; a smile spread from ear to ear.

"Isn't God good?" she exclaimed. "I'm going back to Asia!"

Ezra looked at the tiny woman beside him. So small, yet so capable. Admiration showed in his eyes as he murmured, "God is indeed good."

They weren't going straight to Hong Kong. Oh, no! They planned to take two weeks to reach their new home. After all, this was their honeymoon. First a few days in warm Honolulu, then a visit to Tokyo—during a snowstorm as it turned out! After that Florence had her first glimpse of Korea.

Ezra had friends in Korea, and Florence was surprised to find that she did, too. Dr. and Mrs. Robert Burgess met them at the airport in Seoul. They had worked with Ezra in Taiwan years before. Treva Burgess had also worked with Florence back at the St. Helena Hospital. Dr. George Rue's wife, Grace, had worked with Florence in the San Fernando Valley before either of them were married. What a joy it was to catch up with old friends!

Taipei, Taiwan, was their next stop. They stayed with Pastor and Mrs. Milton Lee. Ezra had watched both Milton and his wife grow up from childhood in the mission field. Now Milton was the speaker for the Chinese *Voice of Prophecy* radio broadcast. The program was aired from Taiwan now, carrying the good news of Jesus' second coming behind the Bamboo Curtain.

The very first morning after arriving in Taipei, Florence asked Helen Lee if she would take her to see her old friend Giang Lan. Just then the telephone rang, and someone asked for Florence. Florence took the phone wonderingly. Who would call her here? Giang Lan didn't even know she was in town yet.

"Hello?"

"Florence, this is Lucy."

"Lucy! You're in Taipei? I thought you wouldn't be here yet."

"I wouldn't miss this for the world. I've been in contact with Giang Lan, and we want to get together—the three of us. How does that sound?"

Florence laughed out loud with happiness and anticipation. "You just say when and where, and I'll be there."

So the three old friends met and talked about old times and God's ever-present blessings. It was as though they had never been separated. They reminded each other of the Christmas Day in 1920 when they had been baptized together in the freezing water of the East River in Wai Chow.

"And then the sun came out, remember?" Florence said.

"Yes, I remember," Lucy replied dreamily. "It seemed that God was smiling on us."

"And do you remember my baby sister?" Giang Lan asked. "Remember how sick she was? She had grown so weak, it appeared that she had stopped breathing. People said she was dead."

"I remember," Lucy said. "Your folks had even called the undertaker."

"Yes," Florence chimed in. "You weren't at church, so I convinced my mother to go with me to your house in the afternoon, remember?"

"How can I forget," Giang Lan said with a gentle smile. "There we were—the funeral ceremony was already started. And your mother walked in and looked around. Then she suddenly reached for my sister's hand."

Giang Lan paused a moment before she continued. "I'll never

forget that day. Your mother suddenly exclaimed, 'This baby isn't dead! Look! She's breathing. Get me a bucket of warm water.'

"She held my sister in the water for about fifteen minutes, praying out loud for God to heal her. Then my little baby sister took a deep breath and began to cry. I've never heard a sound more beautiful than that cry."

The friends talked happily all afternoon. Before they separated, they exchanged addresses and vowed never to lose track of each other again.

Florence knew that once she and Ezra reached Hong Kong, they wouldn't get away again for at least a year. So the last stop before Hong Kong was the one Florence looked forward to the most eagerly. Four hours after the plane left Taipei, Florence pressed her face against the window, watching Saigon emerge from the mist.

In the terminal, they gathered their things and went through customs. Turning to the exit doors, Florence thought she glimpsed a familiar face. As she neared the exit, more familiar faces appeared. Tears of joy flowed down her cheeks when she saw them all—her whole hospital family. Fifteen years had passed since she had left Saigon, but these dear friends still loved her! They threw sweet-smelling flower leis around Florence's and Ezra's necks and hugged and kissed them both. What a wonderful homecoming it was!

Soon Florence and Ezra were winding their way past sights that were familiar to Florence. She exclaimed at them all. At last, they stood before the Saigon Adventist Hospital, housed for now in the United States Military Hospital building. They were taken to the VIP room and made comfortable.

Florence was anxious to see the old hospital building and the Mission office and the press. Most of all, however, she wanted to see the new hospital, which was finally being built, and the mansion where she and Ervin had spent the last week of their stay in Vietnam before they had left to go to America.

Florence was telling Ezra the story of how they were able to purchase the land for the new hospital when someone knocked on their door. Two old friends had come to take them out to dinner. They drove to Cholon to a Buddhist restaurant, and then they climbed three flights of stairs to a banquet room. And there they were again—her hospital family, plus a few other dear friends. How Florence loved these people!

Florence and Ezra spent three wonderful days in Saigon. Before they left, Florence promised to return the next year to cut the ribbon at the opening of the new hospital. She had no way of knowing that she wouldn't be allowed to return; that, in fact, she would never again meet with these dear people in Saigon.

Ezra and Florence were soon airborne once more. Their honeymoon was ending, and they were on the way to their new home. Their work in Hong Kong was about to begin. As the plane flew into the approach pattern, Florence felt excitement building in her. It seemed that every light in Hong Kong—from the boats in the harbor to the skyscrapers on the mountain top—was lit. They glowed like a million diamonds sparkling their welcome.

Before long the Longways stood in the lengthy line awaiting their turn at the immigration desk. When their turn finally arrived, the officer took their passports and flipped through the pages of first one, then the other. Then she looked at them—a long steady look. Then she looked through the passports again. After that she rifled through a stack of papers.

"Is anything wrong?" Ezra asked. "It's all been arranged. We are going to be living and working here in Hong Kong."

The officer looked sternly at him from under her black brows. "Then where is your residence permit? Where is your work permit?"

Oops! Someone in America had failed to get the required permits into their passports, and they themselves hadn't noticed. Now what? Half an hour passed, then an hour, and still they couldn't get permission to enter Hong Kong. Officials questioned them, discussed the problem with each other, and consulted their superiors. Finally the immigration officer gave them a twenty-four-hour permit. (The following day Ezra went to immigration headquarters in Hong Kong and got the official permits they needed.)

It was almost ten o'clock at night before they were able to leave the immigration desk, collect their bags, and pass through customs into the waiting area. And there Florence stood stock still, rapidly blinking back tears. The lobby was packed with hundreds of people! A huge banner on two poles towered above them. It read: WEL-

COME, ELDER AND MRS. LONGWAY! Flashbulbs popped, and people pushed forward to greet them—all smiling and talking at once!

The first person to reach Florence was Lillian Hung, her outpatient department nurse of Saigon days and childhood friend from Wai Chow. "Welcome to your new home, Lotus Blossom," she cried, hugging Florence.

Next was Lillian's sister, Rose, and her husband, Pastor Lo Hing So, the principal of the Boundary Street School. Then followed a procession of many others that she knew from many places in Asia. A charming little girl presented Florence with a huge, colorful bouquet of red roses, yellow chrysanthemums, and tiger orchids, a gift from the Hong Kong-Macao Mission workers. And still more bouquets were showered upon Florence—until her arms were so full that she looked around for Ezra to help hold them. She soon found him in a circle of his own friends from past years, being congratulated on his marriage.

She was just handing some of the flowers to him when her eye caught two dearly loved faces—Pastor and Mrs. Milne. Florence could control her tears no longer. Big drops cascaded down her cheeks.

It took more than an hour to greet all the people who had come to welcome them. Every few minutes someone else would call out, "Lotus Blossom! It's so good to see you again!" The Milnes' car waited for them outside the airport, but they had a hard time getting away. Old friends wanted to talk.

Paul Hung held the door for Ezra and Florence as they climbed into the back seat of the Milnes' car. Then he leaned in and announced, "Next Sunday night we are having a proper welcome dinner for you, so don't make any other plans."

As the car pulled away from the curb, Alma Milne chuckled, "I feel like we are sneaking the bride and groom away! What a welcome they gave you—and this is only the beginning!"

Mrs. Milne spoke the truth. Every evening for weeks, they were invited out for supper with groups of friends. The crowning event was indeed the "Welcome Dinner."

More than a hundred of their closest friends had rented a large banquet hall in a nice restaurant. This was to be no ordinary meal; this was a wedding feast. Florence had been requested to wear her wedding dress. A table in the entry was covered with a red silk cloth. A pheasant

Elder and Mrs. Longway in Hong Kong at the Chinese "wedding" given them by their friends there.

and a dragon, symbols of the bride and groom, were embroidered in the center of it. Then each guest signed his or her name on the silk with a Chinese brush pen and black ink.

Ezra and Florence were led to the table of honor. It was draped with a red tablecloth—even the chairs were red. On the wall behind the table was a large Chinese character that stood for "double blessing," a traditional wedding wish. Red corsages for both Ezra and Florence and a bouquet of pink rose buds completed the bridal arrangements—for the moment.

Many people stood and gave speeches of welcome. Different ones told stories of Florence's childhood days. One doctor showed pictures of her when she was a teenager—to the delight of everyone present. About halfway through the banquet, Lillian and Rose approached Florence. "Come with us," they said, pulling out her chair.

"Where are we going?" Florence asked as she arose.

"You'll see."

They led her into a small dressing room. "Here," Rose said, "put this on."

She pointed to a gorgeous Chinese wedding gown spread over a chair. They felt like giggling girls again as they helped Florence to put on the new gown.

"We missed your wedding, so we're having one for you tonight, Lotus Blossom," Lillian explained. "Rose and I are going to be your bridesmaids."

How appropriate, Florence thought, that these daughters of the *amah* who had loved and cared for her, these friends of her childhood, should be her bridesmaids. Both women had been born on the compound in Wai Chow. And here they were, sixty-plus years later, together once more. They called Ezra to come and get his bride, and the bridesmaids followed them to the front of the banquet hall. The president of the Hong Kong-Macao Mission stood there waiting to officially welcome them to Hong Kong.

★ ★ ★ ★ ★

Within a few days of this lavish banquet, the Longways were able to move out of the Milnes' guestroom and into their own apartment on the twenty-second floor of one of the skyscrapers that covered the island. Their view of the city and the bay was breathtaking. At night, lights across the bay in Kowloon sparkled and shimmered.

But the honeymoon was over; it was time to get to work. Florence found it delightful to work at the new Hong Kong Adventist Hospital. Often during her lunch hour she walked down Bowen Road, just below the hospital. It was a quiet, peaceful trail through tropical foliage. She loved the wildflowers, birds, and butterflies that surrounded her. And there was always a different view of the city below, with the harbor beyond. Looking across the bay to Kowloon, she could even see the airport and watch planes arrive and depart.

Once in a while, she went a little farther down the trail to a place where she could view the old cemetery below. It had not changed since her sixteenth birthday when she promised God she would return to China. Would she ever get to return to the interior of China? Or would that have to be left to a younger missionary at some future time? Her father would be amazed, she thought, if he could see the progress the gospel had made in the Hong Kong-Macao Mission. It now had thirty-two hundred church members and eighteen churches. There was also a very nice college on Clear Water Bay in Hong Kong, and two modern hospitals gave healing to both the rich and poor. Programs had been developed to train nurses and laboratory technicians. The three mission schools enrolled twenty-eight hundred students. Yes, God's work was growing, but there were still millions who needed to hear about Jesus before He could return.

Ezra and Florence Longway in Hong Kong. Lotus Blossom had returned to China at last!

Ezra and Pastor Milne went out every day soliciting funds for the institution. Florence worked in the clinical laboratory. A sorrowful note in Florence's otherwise-happy world arrived in April 1975 when word came that Saigon had fallen to the communists. Florence would not be returning for a ribbon-cutting now. Sadness crept over her. What would become of her hospital family in Vietnam? "Oh, Lord," she prayed, "please watch over our workers in Vietnam. Hide them, protect them, and keep their faith strong."

After the Longways' first year in Hong Kong, the Mission decided to send Ezra and Florence back to the United States for a month or more each year to solicit additional funds from Chinese people living in America. Because Ezra's eyesight was failing, Florence was paid to be his full-time chauffeur. For the next thirteen years, she drove over four hundred thousand miles, crisscrossing the United States, taking Ezra to visit prospective donors. They raised fifteen million dollars on these trips.

In addition to being a chauffeur, Florence worked on her own little project. Whenever they visited a former missionary who had served in China, she asked to see his or her photo albums. On one trip, they visited the home of Fred Wilbur in Portland, Oregon. Fred was the son of Edwin Wilbur, the Canton missionary who had rescued baby Florence and her mother from Wai Chow about sixty-five years earlier.

While they visited together after dinner, Florence asked, "Fred, by any chance do you have any of your parents' pictures relating to the beginning of the Adventist work in China?"

"I sure do," he replied. "Mother gave me a boxful. I don't know what I'll ever do with them. They do no good in my closet."

"This is a miracle!" Florence declared. "May I see them?"

He left the room and returned with a stack of albums. "If they will be of any use to you, you may keep them, if you like."

"Oh, thank you! I don't know what I'll do with them yet, but the Lord will show me. Somehow they ought to be shared."

★ ★ ★ ★ ★

The fifty-second General Conference Session of Seventh-day Adventists was held in Vienna, Austria, in July 1975. At one of the meetings, Pastor Ezra Longway was honored as the missionary with the longest record of continuous service in the denomination—sixty-eight years in China! Florence was excited and thrilled to stand beside her husband as he received the plaque. Only Ellen White had served the church longer, with seventy years of continuous service.

Earlier in his mission career, Ezra had completed the five-year Chinese language course. He had learned Chinese so well that he ultimately translated twenty-six of Ellen White's books into the Chinese language, including her morning watch books for daily devotions. During the dark days in China when the national workers were allowed no contact with the outside world, these books gave them encouragement and a sense of belonging to a worldwide church. Because of this, the faith of many remained strong.

Years passed. Florence and Ezra finally moved back to the United States—to Angwin, California—to enjoy their long-deferred and well-deserved retirement. Then in the spring of 1987 Ezra was diagnosed with terminal cancer. One morning, following his lifelong custom, he arose at four o'clock to go to his office and work on his translation projects. A few hours later, he walked into the kitchen and put his arms around Florence.

"My dear," he said, "my last book is finished; my lifework is done." The next morning Ezra didn't get out of bed. He remained bedfast for the next few months.

One day in August 1987, Florence went to Ezra's bedside to be comforted. She had just received word that Alma Milne, the mentor of her young womanhood, had died. During the thirteen years that Florence and Ezra were in Hong Kong, Florence had cared for the aging Milnes as if she were their daughter. Now she was concerned for Pastor Milne.

On the morning of September 24, 1987, eight days after his ninety-second birthday, her beloved Ezra died. He was finally released from his pain and suffering to wait for the call of Jesus, the Life-Giver.

★ ★ ★ ★ ★

Six months after Ezra's death, Florence was alone in her Angwin home when the silence was broken by the ringing telephone.

"Hi, Mother," Billy's voice boomed over the wires. "How would you like some company?"

"I'd love it! Are you coming over soon?"

"Actually, both Bunny and I want to come see you—together. We'll come over Thursday evening, OK? So lay in the supplies, you know I love your cooking."

Florence prepared all their favorite foods, and they enjoyed a lively meal. But Florence sensed that there was something more to come—a serious reason for their visit. She knew that Bunny had kept in close contact with her father over the years, and that lately she had been helping in Ervin's office in Sacramento. Florence wondered what was coming.

Finally Billy blurted out, "Mother, we want to talk to you about Father. You know he had heart surgery a while back."

"And, Mother," Bunny added, "he just hasn't been able to regain his health since then."

Billy leaned forward. "Would you be willing to come with us to visit him?"

Florence paused a moment, her mind quickly going back over the years. She took a deep breath and spoke, "Why, yes, I would be happy to do it—if he still would like to see me. Anything you want me to do, I'll go along with."

"We think it would be fun to get the whole family together at a Chinese restaurant in Placerville," Billy said.

Florence smiled. "That sounds like a wonderful idea."

So the plan was worked out. Ervin didn't know Florence was coming. But when he saw her getting out of the car, he came over and gave her a big hug.

"I'm so happy to see you again," he said quietly.

After that, the four of them shared a number of family get-togethers at both Billy's and Bunny's homes. Often they looked at old slides or photos of bygone days, happier days.

One time Billy brought Ervin to Angwin to see Florence's home. She made a meal of his favorite dishes. It seemed like old times for both of them. During the evening Chi Sau and her husband Thoi Duong, their helpers in their Saigon home, stopped in to greet Ervin. At the end of the evening, Florence found it hard to say goodbye. She couldn't know it then, but it would be the last time she would see Ervin alive.

Several weeks went by, and Florence heard that Ervin had been hospitalized for heart complications. Then on the morning of September 22, 1988, Bunny telephoned.

"Mother, Daddy passed away last night in his sleep. I was sitting beside him, just holding his hand."

Florence immediately went to Sacramento to be with her children. Ervin had arranged for an Adventist minister to officiate at the funeral service. And at the service, Ervin was praised for being the pioneer doctor who had started the first Adventist medical work in Vietnam. Some of the members of the Vietnamese church nearby attended, along with their pastor.

After the service was over, Ervin's nurse came over to where Florence was standing. "I have something to tell you," she said. "Not long before Dr. Winton died, he asked me to tell you that he had made everything right with his heavenly Father. He said, 'Tell Florence I was ready to go.' "

Tears of joy mingled with Florence's tears of sadness. She looked forward to the resurrection morning when she would meet all the loved ones she had lost over the years. She reveled in that hope.

A few days after Ervin's funeral, Florence began to feel listless—and useless. "Help me, Lord," she prayed. "What am I to do now? How can I be of service to You? I am seventy-nine years old, but I can't just sit in a rocking chair, can I? Please, Lord, I need a work to do!"

CHAPTER TWENTY-TWO

Come Quickly, Lord Jesus

Two weeks later, Florence boarded a plane for Hong Kong. Word had come that Pastor Milne was ill. He needed help, but he had spent his life working in China, and he didn't want to leave Asia now. So Florence would be the daughter he never had. She would take care of him. God had given her a work to do—at least for the three months before her visa expired.

For Florence, it was a lonesome trip. She was used to having Ezra by her side. But when she met Elder Milne at the airport and saw his smile, she knew she was doing the right thing.

They soon settled into a routine. Florence found plenty of time to visit with old friends.

Late one Sunday evening, she returned to her room to find three messages on her door. One was a letter from Bunny with news about the grandchildren. The second was from a friend who left her telephone number. But the third was a telegram.

"What could be wrong at home?" she asked herself. Her hands trembled as she tore open the envelope and read: DOROTHY PASSED AWAY THIS MORNING STOP KENNETH.

Dr. Kenneth Fisher had been a fellow student at both PUC and the College of Medical Evangelists in Loma Linda, California. Dorothy was also a dear friend.

After medical school and a stint in the army, the Fishers had been asked to help pioneer the Montemorelos Adventist Hospital in Monterrey, Mexico. For five years they labored there while Ervin and Florence were in Thailand and Vietnam. Eventually the Fishers accepted a call to Bella Vista Hospital in Puerto Rico. During their nine years there, they became close friends of Rolland Howlett. Rolland was the president of Antillian College in Puerto Rico. He was the same Rolland Howlett who had given rides to Ervin Winton back in the mid-1940s when Ervin needed a way to get between Loma Linda and La Sierra College.

Eventually Kenneth and Dorothy Fisher had returned to the United States to care for his aging mother. And after a long progressive illness, Dorothy died in their home. *She also sleeps the sleep of those who wait for Jesus' return,* thought Florence.

Florence, of course, wrote to Kenneth and expressed her sorrow at his loss. She encouraged him to keep his faith in Jesus

Florence and Kenneth Fisher, a former fellow student, married on February 24, 1990.

strong. Letters flew back and forth during the next few months.

One day R. M. Milne jokingly said, "Florence, I think you'd better return to the United States. I believe this good doctor has some pleasant dreams ahead for you. And don't worry about me. I'll be all right for a while until you can come back."

What a prophet he was! As events turned out, Florence's brother Sherman and his wife Edith returned from Africa on Thursday, February 23, 1990, and the next morning Florence married Kenneth Fisher in a quiet service in a private home in Loma Linda, California.

Kenneth and Florence made their home in Angwin, California, after a honeymoon in Hawaii. But very soon they were on their way to Hong Kong to care for Pastor Milne. Kenneth had never been to the Far East, so Florence had the delightful task of taking him on trips to introduce him to her old friends and to her old homes.

After their return to California, Kenneth took Florence to Mexico for the fiftieth anniversary of the Montemorelos Adventist University and Hospital. Life was exciting for the couple for nine happy years. They were pleased to find Kenneth's old friend Rolland Howlett and his wife, Soletha, now living at PUC. The two couples spent many pleasant hours together.

Soletha began to show symptoms of Alzheimer's. Then Kenneth was diagnosed with cancer. Soletha Howlett died on March 1, 1999, and on May 24 Kenneth closed his eyes for the last time. Both are waiting for the call of the Life-Giver. Florence didn't grieve as much as she might have—she counted her blessings instead. God had given her so many good things and so many good people. She could only praise Him. At age eighty-eight, she expected to be the next one laid to rest.

Suddenly, bubbly, enthusiastic Florence lost her ability to walk. Bedridden and frustrated, she had a hard time staying idle. She wasn't used to being taken care of. Sherman and Edith had returned from Africa, and they spent a lot of time with her. Bunny had moved to Angwin to help care for Kenneth in his last days. Now she cared for her mother, helping her to get back on her feet.

Over time, a routine developed. Monday and Thursday evenings, Sherman and Edith came to play table games with Florence. Bunny worked full time, so she didn't join them.

One evening Sherman remarked, "We need another player! It's more fun if there are four of us. Why don't you invite your friend Rolland to join us?"

"No," Florence replied. "You phone him."

So Sherman did, and Rolland happily joined in game nights. Florence's health continued to improve, and the game nights continued. The friendship between Florence and Rolland grew.

On October 21, 1999, Rolland asked Florence to share his life.

As she prepared for their November wedding, Florence's head was in a whirl. Was this really true? Was God really giving her a fourth wedding and providing someone special to share her life? She and

Rolland had both spent part of their missionary experiences in pioneering educational and medical work in old French Indo-China. So it was natural that they decided to have some Vietnamese touches to their wedding. The last president of the Vietnam Mission before Saigon fell came to Angwin and performed the wedding ceremony in Rolland's home. They had Vietnamese music and a reception in the PUC dining commons with a delicious Oriental meal.

On November 21, 1999, Florence married Rolland Howlett, also a retired missionary.

November 21, 1999, seemed like a beautiful dream to the bride and groom. They had known each other for fifty-three years, and now God had brought them together to spend their sunset years at dear old PUC. They honeymooned in England with Rolland's two daughters. Then they returned to PUC and began a new life together.

Rolland and Florence Howlett receiving the PUC Honored Pioneer award in April 2004, from Richard Osborn, PUC president, and Ron Stretter, PUC Alumni president.

At PUC's 2001 homecoming, Florence and Rolland received the Weniger Award for Excellence. Then, at the 2004 homecoming, they were given the Honored Pioneer award. The alumni association went to great lengths to keep this second award a secret. As volunteers with the alumni association, the Howletts had been involved with the preparation of the homecoming programs. But in 2004, they were not invited so they would not see the printed program. A friend remarked he had heard they were to be honored.

Eventually, they obtained a program. It said the award was to be given between the Sabbath School and worship services on homecoming weekend. But when they arrived for the Pioneer Luncheon on Friday, they were seated at a reserved table. "Reserved for whom?" they asked.

Then in came Florence's son from Montana and her daughter from Angwin with two of her daughters and family from Placerville, California, plus Rolland's daughter from Boise, Idaho—eleven in all. What a surprise! Ron Stretter, Alumni Association president, read the citation for the award, and college president Richard Osborn presented the cut-glass plaque recognizing Florence and Rolland Howlett as Honored Pioneers for their love and devotion to PUC. That evening at the President's Circle banquet, Florence received a crystal PUC pitcher as the only one present from her class of 1933. This was one of the happiest moments of their lives.

★ ★ ★ ★ ★

Every morning Florence and Rolland Howlett praise God for His goodness to them. Florence turned ninety-four on October 16, 2004, and Rolland is just a few years behind her. But there is still no rocking chair for either of them. They have health, friends, hobbies, and worthwhile work to do. They enjoy camping with the El Dorado Nature Club in northern California; they go bird watching; they prepare Chinese or Vietnamese meals for college students from overseas; they do volunteer work for the PUC Alumni Office. And, of course, they still play table games.

Rolland takes stamps that are donated to the Voice of Prophecy and prepares them for resale. In 2003, he prepared 73,798 stamps for the VOP. Rolland is also asked to speak at nearby churches, and Florence happily accompanies him.

Just a few years ago, Florence had a phone call from Elder Samuel C. S. Young of the General Conference headquarters in Washington, D.C.

"Florence," he said, "I have a project I have wanted to do for a long time. And I need your help. I want to publish a book on the history of Adventism in China. November 15, 2002, will mark one hundred years since the arrival of the first missionaries in China. There will be a grand centennial celebration in Hong Kong. Will you write the stories of the lives of the early pioneers? You grew up with them and know them better than any of us. And I understand you have many pictures you've been collecting. We will need those also. It will take a lot of your time, but I will greatly appreciate your help. Will you do it?"

"I would be honored," Florence replied without hesitation "to do anything for the work in my beloved China."

In the end, Florence wrote twenty-six chapters of the 943-page, two-volume book, *100 Years of Adventism in China*. The manuscript was finished and the book was printed in Hong Kong just in time for the centennial. The first copy was presented to Elder Jan Paulsen, president of the General Conference of Seventh-day Adventists.

100 Years of Adventism in China reached the Loma Linda University Alumni Office during the summer of 2003. The volumes contain pictures of most of the very early pioneers, and many of them are alumni of the College of Medical Evangelists. But only a very select group of people in America can read the book—it is written in Chinese! Plans are being made to translate the volumes into English.

Florence and Rolland are grateful to their heavenly Father for their lovely retirement home, surrounded by woods and flowers, where an occasional deer walks through and birds sing every day. Each day they thank God for the privilege of having been missionaries in foreign lands. And they reflect on the joy they've had serving the Lord— a joy they still have as they continue to serve their Master.

Now they look forward to the day when Jesus will come to take them to their heavenly home, along with those with whom they were able to share the gospel message.

"Come quickly, Lord Jesus! Come quickly," is their prayer.

If you enjoyed this book, you'll enjoy these as well:

Though Bombs May Fall
Penny Young Sook Kim, Richard A. Schaefer, Charles Mills. The extraordinary story of George Henry Rue, a Seventh-day Adventist missionary doctor who left a lucrative medical practice in the U.S., to serve the Korean people during the war years. It is a story that takes you into the heart of a beautiful land during its darkest days, revealing the lives of many determined individuals who wrenched success from tragedy.
0-8163-1963-4. Paperback.
US$10.99, Can$16.49.

Prisoner for Christ
Stanley M. Maxwell with *Robert Huang.* In the tradition of Stanley Maxwell's popular *The Man Who Couldn't Be Killed*, ***Prisoner for Christ*** is another compelling true story of how God sustained Pastor Robert Huang in a notorious Shanghai prison.
0-8163-2054-3. Paperback.
US$13.99, Can$20.99.

I Will Die Free
Noble Alexander with *Kay D. Rizzo.* Falsely accused of conspiracy to assassinate Castro, Noble Alexander would spend the next twenty-two years as a political prisoner in one of the most inhumane and brutal prison systems on earth. *I Will Die Free* tells the remarkable story of a young pastor's determined fight to stay alive and remain faithful to his Lord inside the very gates of hell.
0-8163-1044-0. Paperback.
US$9.99, Can$14.99.

Order from your ABC by calling **1-800-765-6955**, or get online and shop our virtual store at **www.adventistbookcenter.com**.
• Read a chapter from your favorite book
• Order online
• Sign up for email notices on new products

Prices subject to change without notice.